# PRAISE FOR
# IT WAS YOUR RETIREMENT, ALL ALONG

"Success in life and success toward retirement are the same. It's not how much money you make, it's your attitude toward developing your retirement plan. Brett Goldstein and Gary Spinell outline a step-by-step plan to not only develop your retirement plan, but also your life plan. Being in the business of helping individuals and companies improve performance and results, I know the methods that Brett and Gary outline, works. It's all about taking personal responsibility, developing your plan and working the plan. Brett will help you accomplish all three!"

—Steve A Klein - CEO
Professional Development Center
PlayMakers Talk Show

"Brett and Gary have written in a plain nontechnical language that engages the reader. Much of their information on the history of retirement plans was new to me, so it was interesting to learn the background on these plans. The chapter on patience and saving for the future ought to be an eye opener for a lot of people."

—Ventriloquist and Comedy Magician Joe Libby
www.joelibby.net

"Wow! It Was Your Retirement All Along is Eye opening! It's an easy read. The information is easy to understand, makes sense, and seems easy to apply. A must read for everyone living in America that wants to enjoy their golden years."

—Justin Tranz, Hypnotist
www.justintranz.com

Brett and Gary brings a fresh and contemporaneous outlook to the project of saving for retirement. It's an attitude shift that taken seriously can transform your life.

—Bonnie Lee E.A.,
Author of "*Taxpertise The Complete Book of Dirty Little Secrets*"

"Brett and Gary have nailed it.! Their insights concerning the perception of saving, and their simple yet effective strategies for changing those perceptions, can radically increase the probability that you will be fully prepared for your retirement. This book is filled with great information. Brett is also a great public speaker, and if you ever get the chance to see and hear him in person, take it!!"

—Anthony Galie Author, Speaker, And Psychotherapist

# *It Was Your*
# RETIREMENT,
## ALL ALONG

Create the life you desire
with financial planning
and positive thinking.

**BRETT GOLDSTEIN & GARY SPINELL**

*It Was YOUR Retirement, All Along*

Copyright © 2017 Brett Goldstein and Gary Spinell

The opinions expressed in this manuscript are solely the opinions of the author and do not represent the opinions or thoughts of the publisher. The author represents and warrants thats/he either owns or has the legal right to publish all material in this book.

An easy to understand guide on how to create your retirement! All Rights Reserved.

This book may not be reproduced, transmitted, or stored in whole or in part by any means, including graphic, electronic, or mechanical without the express written consent of the publisher except in the case of brief quotations embodied in critical articles and reviews.

Cover Photo©

ISBN-13: 978-1975714598
ISBN-10: 1975714598

Library of Congress Control Number: 2017914800 CreateSpace Independent Publishing Platform, North Charleston, SC

# CONTENTS

Foreword . . . . . . . . . . . . . . . . . . . . . . . . . . . . . . . . . . . . . . . . . . 7

Introduction . . . . . . . . . . . . . . . . . . . . . . . . . . . . . . . . . . . . . . 9

Chapter 1   The Way It Used to Be . . . . . . . . . . . . . . . . . . . . . . . . . 12

Chapter 2   Why Everything About Retirement Changed . . . . . . . . . 16

Chapter 3   The Power of Patience . . . . . . . . . . . . . . . . . . . . . . . . . 23

Chapter 4   Only You Are Responsible . . . . . . . . . . . . . . . . . . . . . . 29

Chapter 5   Many Choices, Few Answers . . . . . . . . . . . . . . . . . . . . 37

Chapter 6   Shortcuts Take You
            Nowhere Fast . . . . . . . . . . . . . . . . . . . . . . . . . . . . . . 43

Chapter 7   The Zero Sum Game . . . . . . . . . . . . . . . . . . . . . . . . . . 48

Chapter 8   Change Your Perception, Change Your World . . . . . . . . 54

Chapter 9   It Was You . . . . . . . . . . . . . . . . . . . . . . . . . . . . . . . . . 66

Chapter 10  Your Actions Speak Volumes . . . . . . . . . . . . . . . . . . . . 75

Chapter 11  Saving is Not Automatic . . . . . . . . . . . . . . . . . . . . . . . 82

Chapter 12  The Saving Habit . . . . . . . . . . . . . . . . . . . . . . . . . . . . 88

Chapter 13  Do The Work-Create a Plan . . . . . . . . . . . . . . . . . . . . 93

Chapter 14  Putting It All Together . . . . . . . . . . . . . . . . . . . . . . . . 99

Chapter 15  So what's stopping you? . . . . . . . . . . . . . . . . . . . . . . 104

# FOREWORD
## BY DEAN HANKEY

I have something VERY SCARY to tell you… what you are about to read here is well… a bit frightening. You are going to Retire. Yes, at some point in time you will have to stop working. We don't like to dwell on it, but it will happen. When it does, you will have to live on whatever money you have managed to squirrel away.

Despite the certainty of this event, newspaper headline after newspaper headline has been warning us about how unprepared people are for retirement. Unfortunately, we've almost become immune to the headlines and the warnings of our unpreparedness. Most people believe that they will have enough between their IRA, 401k, and Social Security to get by. Statistics show us that what we believe, is not true. The reality is that four out of every ten Americans over the age of 60, will experience poverty at some point in their later years; regardless of their current economic circumstances.

Look, I get it. NO ONE wants to face the harsh truths of our lives… the good, the bad or the ugly. Truth is, if you want all of your financial dreams and desires to come true, you simply MUST have a clear understanding of "Where You ARE" right now so you can set a path to "Where You Want To Be!"

In order to go from where you are to where you want to be, let's chat briefly about your "M.A.P" (Massive Action Plan). Your "M.A.P." is your plan for getting the RESULTS you want, need, and desire most in your life. For any good 'MAP' to be effective, you have to know the Who, Where, When, How and Why.

- Who will you enlist to help you? Financial Advisors? Family members? Accountants?
- Where will you live in your retirement years? Will you have one home? Will you have a vacation home? In what state will you live?
- When do you want to eventually reach this goal. At what age do you want to retire?
- How you will achieve the goal? What strategies will you use?
- Why do you want to achieve this goal?

As you plot out the route of your M.A.P., you will see that there ARE "Good, Better and Even BEST" practices for achievement. Those are all choices we get to make when working with our M.A.P., such as do I buy the latest Smartphone or do I save that money for later? Consider that even if your journey starts out in California and you're traveling to New York, you 'CAN' actually get there by heading due WEST. Heading West to get to New York, is like hopping on the slow boat to China; it's not the BEST option.

Likewise, your "M.A.P." will serve you better as you become more educated about the Who, Where, When, How and Why. What you will find in the pages of this book is that knowledge to help you determine the Good, Better and Even BEST routes to help you plan your M.A.P.

So crack open this book, get out your passport, while Brett Goldstein and Gary Spinell help you create your financial M.A.P.

Serving You and Your Success,<br>
~ Dean Hankey<br>
The Dean Of Success<br>
http://thedeanofsuccess.com/

# INTRODUCTION

The 2015 Retirement Confidence Survey (RCS), conducted by the Employee Benefit Research Institute and Greenwald & Associates, finds that twenty-two percent of workers are now very confident they will have enough money to live comfortably throughout their retirement years.

Contrast that to the 1996 Retirement Confidence Survey, which showed that thirty percent of Americans were very confident that they would have enough money to live comfortably throughout their retirement years.

In the last twenty years, confidence in being able to retire with enough money has declined. That means that only 22 out of 100 people believe they will have enough money to retire. Yet many Americans have not done anything about it. The unfortunate truth is that most people struggle to give up buying something today in order to have enough to retire on comfortably in the distant future. "Distant future" is the key phrase here. Although they realize that they may not have enough money to retire right now, most people still believe that there will be time to figure something out so they can eventually retire, just as their parents or grandparents did.

Jack Zufelt, author of The DNA To Success says,

> "There are so many success gurus out there who claim their techniques will lead you out of the dry, hot desert of mediocrity

*or failure into a promised land of exciting success…to an oasis of bliss and happiness. The trouble is, techniques aren't what led them to their success, and they won't lead you there, either. If all these techniques and formulas actually brought people, the superstar success they're looking for…why are so many people still looking?"*

This book is not filled with same tips or strategies that Jack is speaking about like buying real estate and tax liens. This book will not discuss how to pick a financial advisor, the components of a well-balanced portfolio, or advise you how to maximize your retirement income. All of this information can be found for free at your local library, online, or at the book store.

People are still looking for the answer to saving for retirement, as there appears to be so many obstacles. Wouldn't life be better if those around me just changed to help me? I would have had more money to pay off my bills or save for retirement, if my boss didn't give away my promotion to someone less qualified. If the government would just give me more tax deductions or if I win the lottery, I'd have more money to put my kids through college. I could retire, if the stock market would continue to go up. If all of these things would happen, I could finally get ahead.

This book was written to help you understand that, although it seems like the world is against you, **you have created the situation you are in**. Your beliefs, actions, and even inactions have led you to where you are right now. The good news is you can create a new situation that includes being on the path to saving for retirement. In this book, you will learn that by changing the way you perceive yourself and the world around you, both you and your world will change. The amount of change and how open you are to change is up to you. We need to start by examining where we have been in order to determine how we can begin to make tomorrow everything we want it to be, and regain what we have lost in order to create a new reality.

# CHAPTER 1
## THE WAY IT USED TO BE

Like a lot of people, you may have visions of retiring at age 65 or 70. You might expect that when you do retire, you'll spend your time traveling, playing games like golf or tennis, and living in a nice house in a warm climate. Unfortunately, that's just not the reality facing many retirees today. Nor is it the future retirees should be looking forward to.

Many retirement-aged people are finding they simply can't afford to give up their paycheck. They don't have enough income and must continue to go to work, possibly for another 10 to 20 years longer than they expected. For those who *do* retire, or are forced into retirement after losing a job, Social Security is their major source of income. Unfortunately, that doesn't provide enough to cover even basic expenses.

It's a grim picture, but an accurate one for many seniors. According to the U.S. Department of Health and Human Services Administration on Aging (AoA), more than 3.6 million elderly people were living below the poverty level in 2011. Similarly, a Kaiser Family Foundation state-by-state snapshot of poverty among seniors in 12 states[1], showed they were twice as likely to be below the poverty line than the general population.

It's worth pointing out that those figures *included* Social Security. If it weren't for Social Security, millions more seniors would have been

---

[1] California, Colorado, Connecticut, Hawaii, Massachusetts, Maryland, Minnesota, New Hampshire, New Jersey, Nevada, Wisconsin, and Wyoming.

considered impoverished. Currently, more than half of our country's elderly depend on Social Security for greater than 50% of their income. One-quarter depend on Social Security for a whopping 90% of their income, and 15% count it as *all* of their income. Put together, these figures tell us **that 9 out of 10 seniors are highly dependent on Social Security to meet their regular expenses**. For most retirees, Social Security is barely enough to get by.

Because of the high cost of medical care and other basic expenses like food, taxes, and rent or mortgage expenses, today's retirees are finding they can't survive on what they receive. The AARP estimates that 4 out of every 10 Americans over the age of 60 will experience poverty at some point in their later years; regardless of their current economic circumstances. Because this point is so important, I want to put it another way. At least 40% of all seniors are expected to have retirement incomes of $15,930 per year *or less* during their retirement. In addition, those in their 20's, 30's and 40's worry that there will not be enough money from Social Security by the time they are ready to retire. Hence, our discussion here pertains to those beginning to start savings as well those looking to retire soon.

How did we get to this point? How is it that Americans work for 40 or 50 years – raising kids, paying for college, and saving money for their golden years – yet still wind up retiring in poverty? The big question that everyone wants to know is, what can you do now in your 20s, 30s, or 40s, to ensure you won't have to depend on Social Security when you get older?

To answer that question, let's take a step back in time and see how the concept of retirement evolved. In the Colonial era if you were breathing, you were working. Or to put it another way, if you stopped working it was probably because you stopped breathing. There was no retirement, as the average life expectancy was only 38 years.

Things had changed a little by the late 1800s. The Industrial Revolution was well underway and Americans were using steel in everything from engines to train tracks. Along with the assembly line came a realization: Older workers were no longer strong, or fast enough to keep up with the machinery they depended on; they were slowing down production. Factory managers and corporate decision-makers realized they needed to get older workers out of the way so they could replace them with younger, faster employees.

Companies were uncomfortable with the idea of putting loyal older workers into the streets to starve. To solve the problem of laying off older workers, without throwing them into extreme poverty, employers created pension plans in the 1920s. These newly created pension plans allowed corporations to eliminate older workers, secure in the knowledge that they would have enough money to survive.

This was undoubtedly a positive step for those who could no longer work, but it was an incomplete solution. Pensions were funded on an entirely voluntary basis by employers, who were only willing to contribute on their own terms. They reserved the right to change their plans at will, leaving no guarantees for the employees who counted on them. This became evident when the auto company Studebaker declared bankruptcy.

In 1962, Studebaker was a leading auto firm that had already been around for 110 years. In addition to making cars they also manufactured STP, an oil additive. They were also involved in the aerospace business and were the sole distributors for Mercedes-Benz in the United States. The successful firm had a rich pension plan that boasted retirement benefits for employees. The plan paid out more than $2 every month, which was generous in its time.

By 1963, however, the company owed employees more money than it had in the pension plan. With declining sales, Studebaker could no longer stay in business. Older workers who had been with the company for a long time got a fraction of what they were promised. Newer and younger employees received nothing at all. Their safety net disappeared virtually overnight.

In September 1972, NBC aired a documentary called *Pensions: The Broken Promise*. The program exposed Studebaker, and other companies, by interviewing former employees who explained how they had lost some or all of their pension income. Some had been fired from their jobs, while others had worked for companies that went out of business or mismanaged the pension funds. Even worse, the employees had no recourse as these corporations weren't under any obligation to actually pay the pension benefits they had promised.

Eventually, attention and outcry over the issue became so pervasive that Congress responded to public pressure. Congress held a series of hearings on pension issues and support for pension reform grew significantly. In 1974, President Ford signed the Employee Retirement Income Security Act (ERISA) which, among other things, guaranteed that employees would receive their pensions.

Suddenly, workers started looking forward to retirement. Between the money they got from their former employers and Social Security (which had begun benefiting the elderly a few decades earlier), retirees had a monthly income that couldn't be taken away.

History and progress conspired to bring us to a point where Americans didn't have to save anything for retirement. For a long time, no one retired at all. Retirement came about when employers fired older employees who couldn't keep up with the machines of the industrial age. With the passage of pension reform and Social Security, Americans weren't responsible for their own savings. With a pension in one hand and Social Security in the other, retirement became something to look forward to.

It was a good system for those early retirees who had kept good jobs over the years. However, things were about to change drastically.

# CHAPTER 2

## WHY EVERYTHING ABOUT RETIREMENT CHANGED

In 1978, the Internal Revenue Code was changed and section 401(k) was enacted into law. Under the new guidelines, employee contributions to a retirement account would be taxed differently. Specifically, those funds would be tax-deductible in the years when contributions are made, and not considered as income until withdrawals took place later on.

Employers loved the idea of allowing their workers to contribute to 401(k) plans because it gave them a much more affordable option than providing a pension. No business wanted to end up being the next Studebaker, offering retirement benefits they couldn't actually afford. At the same time, corporations were skeptical that the IRS would allow for these new types of accounts. Section 401(k) was an obscure piece of tax code at the time and it was unclear whether the tax-friendly language would hold up to scrutiny.

Ted Benna, a Philadelphia retirement planner, read the new IRS codes and was the first to create a 401(k) plan. Then, he pressed tax authorities to clarify the legality of these accounts. They did, and a whole new way of saving was born.

Not only did 401(k)s began to replace pension plans at a rapid pace, but they were a major tax deduction by wealthy business owners. The maximum contribution in 1981 was $30,000 (which equates to $82,221 at the time of this writing).

Fearing the government would lose out on more and more tax revenue, as wealthy individuals took advantage of the new 401k, Congress lowered the cap on 401(k) deposits to $7,000 (or $19,185 in today's money). To further prevent the use of 401(k) plans as tax loopholes, Congress further restricted contributions to twenty-five percent of an employee's salary.

For business owners and executives, however, the genie was out of the bottle. The lower contribution ceilings didn't stop corporations from replacing pension plans with 401(k)s. In 1983, there were 175,100 active pension plans in the U.S. By 1993, just a decade later, that number had dropped by fifty-two percent. In that year, there were 154,500 401(k) plans covering 23 million American workers. It took less than a decade from there to reach a point where only 46,000 corporations were offering pension plans in 2001 – a seventy-three percent decrease since 1983.

For employers the appeal of a 401(k) plan was clear. Doing away with pensions meant they no longer had to guarantee a monthly income to retired employees. They could take the responsibility of planning for a worker's later years, including any investment risks, and pass it off to the individual.

While businesses in the 1920s didn't want to fire their older employees and leave them without money, things changed in the subsequent decades. By the late 1990s, because 401k's had shifted the responsibility for saving to employees, executives and shareholders were less concerned whether their workers had enough to retire on or not; that was between the employee and the stock market. This tilt in perspective accompanied a heavier focus on profits, share prices, and employee productivity. Corporations became more about the bottom line and less about employee welfare; as evidenced by the massive layoffs that occurred during the tech bubble in 2001, and again with the catastrophic recession conditions beginning in 2008.

Of course, just because 401(k) laws were favorable to businesses didn't mean they were equally favorable to employees. Some business owners and executives took advantage of the new regulations, to the detriment of millions of individual workers. They wanted productive employees who would show up on time, but they were less concerned about an employee's finances.

There are numerous examples we could examine that show just how painful this transition was for so many people who were unprepared. For the sake of brevity, we'll highlight just a couple of the best known that illustrate the depth of the problem.

In the 1990s, AT&T needed an undersea cable linking the U.S. and Europe. However, the company didn't want to pay for this project out of pocket. So, they turned to Gary Winnick, the founder of a company called Global Crossing, telling him that if he could raise $750 million, AT&T would handle the construction and pay Winnick's firm to utilize the fiber optics. With this assurance in place, Mr. Winnick personally invested $15 million and raised the remainder of the sum in a mere 90 days. A brand-new tech enterprise was born.

By August 1998, Global Crossing was ready to go public and debuted at $9.50 a share. As the internet industry exploded, the stock rose in price rapidly, jumping to $60 per share by 1999. During this time, Global Crossing made the entirety of its matching 401(k) contributions as company stock. Employees were required to hold on to their shares for five years before they could cash out. But, given that it just kept going up and up, few saw any reason to worry.

Eventually, the completely unexpected happened. It was revealed that Global Crossing had engaged in dishonest accounting that inflated their revenues, and that management had gone on an unbridled corporate spending spree. While the CEO was selling off his shares at record highs – and pocketing an estimated $600 million in the process – the business was sinking like a stone. The company's bankruptcy was the fourth largest in America's history, and employees lost nearly all of their retirement savings.

For an even more famous example of corporate misbehavior, we can examine the case of Enron. By 1997, the corporation was the nation's largest wholesale buyer and seller of natural gas and electricity. As with Global Crossing, Enron would only match employee 401(k) contributions in company stock. Workers who wanted to set something aside for their retirement had no other choice, so they did what any sensible investor would do and accepted their shares.

In February 2001, Enron's CEO, Jeffrey Skilling told Wall Street that his company's stock – trading at $80 per share at the time – merited a valuation of $126 per share. Despite his supposedly bullish outlook, it was just eight months later, in October, that the corporation announced it had changed administrators for the 401(k) pension plan. As part of the transition, workers would find their accounts were locked for a period of 30 days. Legal guidelines prevented them from selling any stock they might own during the switch from one provider to another.

The timing of the decision raised suspicions, and five days later Enron announced that the government was launching an investigation into their business dealings. Share prices began to drop, but employees couldn't sell because of the 30-day freeze that was mandated by law. A few weeks later, on November 8, Enron announced that it had omitted $591 million in losses in filings, and had also failed to disclose an additional $628 million in liabilities from its accounting reports. At that point, Enron shares plummeted. Within a period of six weeks, the company's 11,000 employees lost around $1 billion in their 401(k) plans.

CEO Jeffrey Skilling knew all along that the company had hidden millions upon millions of dollars from its accounting reports just to drive up share prices. Did he care that his workers had 60% of their retirement savings invested in Enron stock? No. He only cared about his own financial gain. With the knowledge that an eventual collapse was on the way, he personally sold nearly $60 million of his own company stock prior to the free fall.

Skilling was eventually charged with 35 counts of fraud and sentenced to 24 years in a federal prison. However, the $1 billion lost in employee 401(k) plans wasn't covered by insurance, and was never recouped by those who were counting on it for their futures. They became the new Studebaker employees, watching their retirement savings be completely wiped out and having no recourse. Although laws had been changed to protect pensions, those safeguards didn't apply to 401(k)s.

The losses suffered by the employees of Enron and Global Crossing highlight extreme examples, but they point to a larger lesson. Corporations tend to do a much better job of looking out for their management teams and shareholders than they do their employees, particularly when it comes to safeguarding their retirement savings.

Unfortunately, despite the hard-to-miss headlines that come with each new scandal, the experiences are forgotten all too quickly, and warning signs continue to be missed. Employees of "blue-chip" companies routinely invest the bulk of their retirement savings in company stock, despite available evidence that suggests it is unwise for them to do so. Most workers assume they are better protected from the risks of fraud and mismanagement than they actually are. For instance, the collapse of Enron occurred in 2001. However, regulations weren't put in place to stop a similar situation from occurring until five years later.

There was a time when it would have been almost unthinkable for a corporation to jeopardize an employee's retirement. However, the current "every man for himself" economic climate we live in has warped corporate culture and thinking. Companies aren't interested in providing for the retirement of their workforce anymore, much less guaranteeing it. Of course, not every executive is willing to lie, cheat, or steal to make a profit. That doesn't mean you should trust them to make the best possible decisions for your future.

No matter where you look there are corporations cutting employee pay, slashing benefits, reducing options, and taking away bonuses; all to drive higher profits. Employers are outsourcing jobs overseas, reducing the hours of non-exempt staff members, and hiring younger employees who require less in salary and benefits than older workers. This has all happened amid a huge shift in wealth for the top one percent of individuals in the U.S.; many of whom represent senior management within publicly traded companies. In the same way that you can no longer be assured your employer will keep paying you to do a great job, neither can you count on the notion that they'll keep on matching your 401(k) and guide you into a comfortable retirement.

Your parents, grandparents, and great-grandparents came from an age where they didn't have to save for their golden years. Everything was provided for them, so long as they could hold on to a good job. Even if they *had* saved a chunk of money to retire with, there wasn't much to save for. The average life expectancy for a male in 1980 was 70 years, and a female could expect to make it to the age of 77. That meant most seniors spent less than 10 years in retirement. That's not a lot of time to save for.

In contrast, the U.S. Census Bureau forecasts that the 65+ population will double between the years 2010 and 2050. The number of people aged 80 and older will nearly triple, and the population of nonagenarians and centenarians – men and women living in their 90s and 100s – will *quadruple*.

In many ways, our expectations have not caught up with medical technology or the realities of today's economy. Many of us still expect to retire at the age of 65, just as our parents and grandparents did. However, we are rapidly seeing that magic number increasing as many men and women have no choice but to work longer; both because of reduced financial health and the potential for a much longer lifespan. You could work until the age of 75 and still have a good chance of living for another 20 years after you quit. Someone who is in their 30s today could easily imagine living to be 100 years old.

Advances in medical care have certainly allowed us to live longer. The downside to living longer is the necessity to save more money for retirement. It's one thing to save money for retirement, which was expected to last 10 years. It's a different story when you have to save money that will last you 20 or 30 years beyond your working career. Add to that the rapidly rising costs of college expenses, health care, basic living needs and it's not hard to see why people are outliving their retirement savings.

As you look ahead in time, your retirement mantra should be, "How much money do I need to have at retirement? How much can I save over the next 30 to 50 years to meet my retirement goals?" Once you start thinking in those kinds of terms, the next question becomes the most critical one of all: *How can you save money for retirement NOW?*

As you'll see in the next chapter, the most obvious answer is one we tend to ignore.

# CHAPTER 3
## THE POWER OF PATIENCE

In June of 2014, a Vermont man named Ronald Read passed away at the age of 92. During his career, Ronald had worked as a janitor and gas station attendant. Despite his low income jobs, the *Wall Street Journal* reported that when he died he left $8 million behind.

How was Ronald Read – a low-income earner by any American standard – able to amass that kind of fortune? He used the power of patience. Mr. Read started investing on January 13, 1959 when he bought 39 shares of Pacific Gas & Electric for $2,380. From there, he just kept investing when he could.

Ronald bought those first shares when he was 38 years old. Unlike a lot of today's investors, he didn't look to make a few quick bucks from a stock tip. Instead, he spent the next fifty-six years quietly and patiently putting away his savings. It couldn't have been easy. Ronald would have seen the stock market decline by more than ten percent in 1996, lose eight percent of its value in 1969, and drop a staggering thirty percent between 1973 and 1974. He would have sat through big losses again between 2000 and 2002, and once more 2008.

No matter what happened, Ronald didn't stop investing despite wars, gas shortages, inflation, recessions, and other grim news. He knew what so many seem to have forgotten: building real wealth generally isn't something that happens quickly. As a society, we need to learn to be more patient with our investments. We need to figure out our financial goals, and then make plans to reach them.

It's easy to see the value of planning in other parts of our lives. Nearly 100,000 commercial flights operate in the United States every day. Even though the routes aren't new and there are numerous controllers watching every flight via radar at all times, pilots still go through the exercise of planning every journey in exacting detail. They study terrain, weather, fuel requirements, and even the weight of the aircraft itself. During the flight they continually check their position to see if they've deviated from the planned course, making necessary corrections as they go along.

Pilots do that because they know that, despite all the technology and safeguards that are in place, they could easily end up at the wrong destination if they aren't careful. Or worse, they could run into trouble and not have an immediate course of action that would take them to safety. Would you board a flight under those conditions?

Although retirees can be expected to live 20 or 30 years in retirement, they simply hope that they can save enough for retirement or that Social Security will be enough to live on. It's safe to say that many of us have never made a plan that's even as remotely detailed as the ones that are made for us when we take a three-hour flight. Pilots do more planning for a quick three-hour trip, than we do for something that will last 20 or 30 years.

To understand why, let's look at a few pertinent numbers. Suppose your desire was to have a retirement income of $50,000 per year. Let's assume you were retiring today, and would live another 20 years, earning seven percent on the savings you had in the bank. Under those conditions, you would need to have $714,000 in your retirement account to meet that goal.

Most readers probably don't have that kind of money saved, and aren't on track to accumulate it. Working backward, a 45-year-old who contributes $4,100 per year to their retirement plan (or $78.85 per week) would need to earn thirteen percent on their investments every year to reach that goal. However, most won't be able to generate that sort of return, and trying to do so would involve some big risks.

If we set our sights a bit lower, the same 45-year-old could begin saving $100 per week and earning seven percent on their money. If they were willing to delay their retirement until the age of 70, they could accumulate $324,000 over that time frame. Assuming they had paid off their home and could supplement their savings with Social Security, it could be enough to cover basic necessities.

It doesn't take any complicated math to arrive at these figures. Anyone can verify them, and most people reading this book could manage to save $100 a week, and perhaps much more, if they were to make their retirement a priority. But, how can we expect the average American to put away enough to accumulate $300,000 – much less the amount they will actually want for a truly comfortable retirement – when most people aren't saving at all?

According to a recent study by Torsten Slok, chief international economist at Deutsche Bank, nearly half (forty-seven percent) of American households don't save *any* of their money. Even scarier, that percentage has increased by seven percent since 2001. As things have gotten harder, and more uncertain, we are saving less instead of more.

That's unfortunate, because the numbers we've provided don't tell the whole story. For one thing, they fail to factor in inflation. Even if you aren't completely fluent in economics, you know that things cost more now than they used to. You might have had grandparents who reminded you that candy bars used to cost a nickel, even though they often sell for a dollar in today's world. Inflation means a hard-earned buck will no longer buy you 20 chocolate bars. It also means that a dollar saved for retirement today won't get you as much in the future as it does now.

What will $50,000 in yearly income be worth in 20 or 30 years? No one can answer that question with complete clarity. However, what we *can* do is look back in history and say that $50,000 in 1983 would have been equivalent to $118,969.92 in 2015. In another 20 years, you might need $106,000 annually just to maintain the same kind of lifestyle you would get on $50,000 today.

Additionally, it's important to factor in the high costs of healthcare. According to the Employee Benefit Research Institute, most retirees will need $376,000 just to cover health insurance premiums, co-pays, deductibles, and prescriptions during their golden years. This figure doesn't include nursing home costs, which can be substantial. Estimates from Genworth Financial Inc. suggest the national average cost of a private room in a nursing home is currently $92,370 per year. A semi-private room goes for $82,125, and a place in an assisted living community costs $43,539.

Once we factor those figures in, the amounts needed to retire comfortably change quite a bit. If we add inflation and healthcare into our estimations, that same 45-year-old will have to save nearly $800 per week, earning seven percent annually, to reach the $1.7 million it would take to maintain their lifestyle in retirement.

Before you start thinking it's hopeless and put this book away, let me remind you that our goal isn't to persuade you to give up. Instead, we want you to understand the reality most Americans are facing and begin to explore some simple solutions.

The first is to put time on your side. Going back to the numbers we have given you, we want to note that someone who is 25 years old today, and plans on retiring at 65, only has to save $125 per week to reach the same target. Waiting from the age of 40 to the age of 45 means you'll have to save an additional $193 *each week* to catch up. The longer you have to work with, the easier things get. There is great power in patience.

We're going to assume that if you started saving for your retirement in your 20s, you don't need this book in the first place. So for everyone else, consider the years you have ahead of you. If you are healthy and productive, you might be able to delay your retirement until age 70 or 75. Doing so could make an enormous difference on your financial situation later.

No matter where you are in your life, though, recognize how important it is for you to begin planning saving money *right now*. If you haven't been putting away as much money as you should, or haven't saved any at all, you're obviously not alone. As we've already stated, nearly half of Americans aren't saving anything, and today's headlines are filled with articles and surveys documenting the financial shortfall many retirees will face in the coming decades.

Many of these individuals will blame the sudden and dramatic declines the stock market has experienced in the last 15 years. But, while the stock market has recouped, most were slow to start investing again, and so they missed out on the biggest gains. Had they taken a slow and steady approach they would have been fine.

The real cause and culprit is that most of us don't have the patience to make or stick to a budget.

We make excuses, but the fact is we are easily swayed to spend our dollars on things that make us feel good about ourselves, or cause others to look at us in a certain way. Most Americans lead very stressful lives. At your job you have deadlines that must be met or you could get fired. Kids must get to their after school activities on top of getting dinner on the table at a certain hour. In order to give ourselves a break from the stress and receive some immediate satisfaction, we engage in buying the latest smart phones, TVs, or tablets. We spend money on complicated coffeemakers, or lattes from chirpy baristas to feel better. We then pay for the items on our credits cards not fully understanding how this makes saving even more of a struggle.

Budgeting and saving is an active discipline. With the beliefs, which we will talk about in another chapter, you can do it. We began this chapter by sharing the example of Ronald Read, who had a critical personality trait that prevented him from living beyond his means and forced him to save money. He accepted the fact that he was responsible for his own actions, and in charge of directing the course of his financial life.

As a society, we have largely lost the sense of being in charge of our own fates. We focus on earning money and spending it to make us happy today. With all of the stress that life brings, we are constantly looking for things to make us happy today. That leaves us ultimately trying to accumulate wealth quickly.

None of us can rely on the government, our employer, or others in our lives to take care of our financial futures. Each of us must take on the individual responsibility of managing and saving for our retirements. No one but you will provide for your golden years. Are you ready to start working to bring your vision to life?

# CHAPTER 4
## ONLY YOU ARE RESPONSIBLE

Dean Hankey is a magician, hypnotist, and entrepreneur. He also happens to be a close friend. At the age of 12, he produced his first magic show. By 16, he was a full time business owner making money for himself. Over the years he's appeared at events for numerous Fortune 500 corporations, not to mention, in some of the most exclusive resorts around the world.

To read that summary of his career, you would assume that his path went straight to the top. The reality is much different. At 22 years old, Dean was homeless and living out of the back of a broken down pickup truck. He had just moved to Los Angeles and, without any business contacts, couldn't find paying gigs for his magic shows. Without a way to perform he couldn't earn any money and without money he couldn't pay his rent. It didn't take long before he no longer had a place to stay.

Dean lived in his truck for a while, but eventually it was towed away by the authorities. Without any money to his name he would often eat at McDonald's. Dean didn't walk into McDonald's to get a Big Mac with a side of fries. Instead he would request free packets of ketchup and some complementary hot water. Then, he would mix the two together to make a depressing version of tomato soup. If he could scrape together a few crackers, it amounted to a hot meal.

Dean's running joke is that he had to climb up the side of the gutter just to be flat broke! Unlike a lot of people who find themselves in difficult circumstances, Dean used his poverty as a motivator. He didn't want to be homeless, and certainly didn't want others to know the conditions he had found himself in.

So, just when things looked most bleak, Dean decided to evaluate his situation and take responsibility for his own life. He recognized that it wasn't anyone else's fault that he was homeless. At the same time he believed he had the ability to change his situation and generate some income.

With that mindset in place, Dean started performing his magic anywhere and everywhere he could get an opportunity. He performed on the streets for tips and gave impromptu demonstrations in restaurants, in exchange for a hot meal. Using his knowledge as a hypnotist, he began adding therapy as a service to help others to get what they wanted, needed, and desired. He felt certain that if he assisted enough people they would begin to return the favor. After eight months of following this plan, he was finally able to earn enough money to find a place to live and push his career further in the right direction.

We mention Dean here because he has perfectly illustrated that each of us has a choice, no matter where we are in our lives. We can take stock of our situation and determine whether our plan has been a success or failure. More importantly, if things haven't been working out the way we would like them to, we should stop trying to lay blame on someone else and find out what we need to do in order to find a solution.

Dean Hankey could have made excuses about the entertainment business, the economy, the job market, or even other performers. He could have complained about the agents and booking managers who wouldn't hire him, or the way TV executives wouldn't return his calls. He didn't do any of that and as a result he's successful today. He looked in the mirror, found the root cause of the problem, and decided to change who he was so he could get different results from the outside world.

Most people who have failed at anything will only blame the individual they see in the mirror as a last resort. To do so, they would have to acknowledge that they need to change their own beliefs and behaviors. They would be forced to admit their approach, thoughts, and decisions have taken them in the wrong direction. Most of us have egos that are far too fragile for that kind of honesty. "It must be someone else's fault," we tell ourselves again and again; even while we continue to fall short.

This isn't just an individual problem but one that plagues our entire society. To understand how pervasive it is, you only have to look at the way politicians play this card again and again when running for office. Men and women who are running for president blame the current president, or maybe the last one, for the problems the nation is facing. In 1976, Ronald Reagan beat Jimmy Carter by asking Americans if they were better off than they were four years ago. If you can't remember that far back, Presidential Candidate Mitt Romney asked Americans the same question about President Obama's handling of the Great Recession which started in 2008

President Obama blamed President George Bush for the worst recession since the Great Depression and Franklin Delano Roosevelt blamed everything on his Republican predecessor Herbert Hoover. It may not be the previous or current Presidents fault, but presidential candidates are happy to blame them anyway.

The same trick has been used again and again during every election year. That's because elected officials know it's an approach that works. Directing the blame to others for the unfortunate circumstances in our lives is easy. It allows us to save face and not admit we've been wrong. It also gives us a fast-and-easy "solution" to our problems that doesn't require any work. If we were to face up to our own shortcomings, it would mean we needed to alter our own behavior and maybe adopt new skills or mindsets. Taking responsibility for ourselves means putting in some hard work and having to exercise patience. Most of us aren't well-programmed for either.

Look around, and you'll see evidence that Americans would haven't accepted responsibility to their lack of saving. Instead of saving money and budgeting, we rely on winning it than saving it. There are dozens of "reality" TV shows devoted to this very phenomenon. Many of them may audition tens of thousands of people, each of whom stand in line for entire days just to get the chance to win a slice of fame and a sum of money. In fact some of them are willing to risk injury, or even their lives, for less than you might think.

At the time of this writing, there is a new program called *Alone* that puts contestants in a remote wilderness, without food, shelter, or companionship, for as long as they can stand. Unless they can build fires, keep dry, and catch or kill something to eat, they are risking death. What is the prize for the person who can endure suffering and loneliness for the longest? Half a million dollars. As we've already discussed, a fraction of what they would likely need to retire.

A researcher named Bernice Kanner once conducted a survey and found that fifty-nine percent of her recipients would shave their head for $10,000. For a cool million, sixty-five percent would live on a deserted island for a year. A mind-blowing sixty-percent would take the blame for a crime they didn't commit and serve six months in jail.

As a society, we are motivated to go to prison for money or live in the wilderness without food and comfort, yet we aren't willing to put away a few dollars from every paycheck. The reason for this odd disparity is that most of us struggle with basic financial concepts and don't understand the way money works. We have unpleasant memories of math class and can't fathom the kinds of complex equations it would take to plan for our retirement.

The situation becomes all the more unfortunate when you consider that, the reality of personal finance concepts are quite simple. If Ronald Read could master the principles needed to amass $8 million, you can, too. The key is to start thinking about money differently, in terms of saving, expenses, and being patient.

In 2014, Americans spent a total of $70.15 billion on lottery tickets, per the North American Association of State and provincial lotteries. To put that number in perspective, it's 10 times the amount spent on music and seven times the amount spent going to the movies. In fact, it was more than the $62.7 billion we spent on *all* other forms of leisure and entertainment combined.

Intellectually, we all realize that the odds of winning the lottery are low. However, buying a ticket is easier than denying yourself the joy of buying something, or educating yourself on the right way to set a budget. Thus, millions of us engage in wishful thinking rather than developing a concrete retirement plan and sticking to it.

Although there are courses available in basic math, finance, and economics, most people never even consider taking them. They could educate themselves online, visit a local college, or even check out some learning options at the library. Despite the fact that the information they need is all around them, a 2015 financial literacy survey by the National Foundation for Credit Counseling showed that forty-one percent of those surveyed graded themselves with a "C," "D," or "F" on the subject of personal finance.

This clearly shows that there is a real need for financial education. Unfortunately, many of the parents who are teaching us about finances would themselves fail, or at least barely pass, a financial literacy test. It's the blind leading the blind.

However, education about retirement planning is not taught in school or at work. Studies have shown that most people learn about personal finances from their parents or other relatives. Many high schools and even middle schools in New York participate in the stock market game. Teams of one to five students invest an imaginary $100,000 in common stocks listed on the New York and American Stock Exchanges and the NASDAQ. The results are printed in the local paper, and the winning team receives a prize.

Some would say that this game makes learning about the stock market fun, since the children are learning about stocks, dividends, how to make trades, and so on. That's true, but they are also learning that the person who has the most money wins. As a result, the game is perpetuating a problem rather than filling an educational gap.

We aren't teaching the kids about diversification and how important it is not to have all of your eggs in one basket. They aren't learning about investing for their futures, or how important it is to spread their money among other investment choices, not just stocks. The students aren't learning how to have a well-balanced portfolio. But they are investing their "pretend money" very aggressively, simply in order to win the game. Would they do that if it were real money?

Clearly there is a real need for financial knowledge, but an even greater need for Americans to assume the responsibility for their own futures. Few of us would be so reckless in other areas of our lives. We value the importance of being educated consumers, and will carefully weigh the pros and cons of our decisions. When facing a serious illness, we will get a second opinion. If it's time to send the kids to college, we schedule visits, take tours, research tuition, demographics, and the prospects for recent graduates. We'll read a dozen *Consumer Reports* and visit several different dealers before buying a new car.

Yet when it comes to one of the most important topics in our lives, one that could affect our day-to-day circumstances for 20 or 30 years to come, we seem perfectly happy to leave things to chance. "I don't know that much about retirement planning," we say. "It's too confusing." Would you rather make excuses, or gain some control over the rest of your life?

Ask anyone what your "Miranda" rights are and they can tell you. They may not be able to recite the whole thing, but most people can remember,

*"you have the right to remain silent, anything you say....".*

People who have never been arrested before can recite this. People who have never been arrested before also know that police need a search warrant before they enter your home. How come we know so much more about criminal law than we do about financial or retirement planning? ***To ensure your financial success, you must take an active role and not stand by while the world changes. You have the ability and power to transform your financial situation no longer being influenced by the actions of others.*** Coming to that one realization can change your life in many different ways.

The author and motivator Jim Rohn makes an excellent point on this subject. He writes: "if you don't design your own life plan, chances are you'll fall into someone else's plan. And guess what they have planned for you? Not much."

**If you don't plan for your own retirement, you have given away your power to create the retirement you desire.** When you don't plan or save for retirement you are forced to accept the government's plan for your retirement, which is to provide you with just enough income to keep you just above the poverty line.

When it comes to retirement, that reward at the end of a long career, it's imperative to recognize that our favorite rich uncle (also known as Uncle Sam) will only provide for a portion of our needs via Social Security, Medicaid, and Medicare. While it's true that our parents and grandparents got help from company pension plans and government programs, we shouldn't expect the same.

Pensions have been replaced by 401(k)s, Social Security is getting squeezed because of funding pressures, and retirement is no longer a right. It's something you have to plan and save for, otherwise you could find yourself working at a job you don't enjoy until you are physically unable to do so. And if that happens, you might find yourself in poverty.

The biblical Proverbs 21:5 tells us: "the plans of the diligent lead to profit as surely as haste leads to poverty." Regardless of your beliefs, that's good advice. Those who take responsibility for their finances and master the concepts behind retirement planning are preparing themselves for a bright future. Those who don't are in for a rough ride.

We hope you'll take this moment to accept responsibility for your own financial future. Once you do, you need to start making smart choices. If you began asking yourself things like: "What are some of the basic steps to save on a regular basis?" Now you're on the right track and are ready to focus on the things that actually matter to your future.

Don't become overwhelmed at this stage in the process. You may begin to look up answers and discover there are Roth IRAs, SIMPLE IRAs, and regular IRAs. You might read about stocks, bonds, and CD rates. You'll be confronted with decisions on insurance, annuities, and other financial products. Rather than worry about which one(s) are right for you at the moment, you need to take the first step.

# CHAPTER 5

## MANY CHOICES, FEW ANSWERS

Let's suppose for a moment that you had decided to take our advice and were feeling enthusiastic about setting up a retirement account. Which of the following might you choose?

- ✓ SEP
- ✓ SIMPLE IRA
- ✓ Roth IRA
- ✓ 401(k)
- ✓ SIMPLE 401(k)
- ✓ Safe Harbor 401(k)
- ✓ Roth 401(k)
- ✓ Defined Benefit Plan
- ✓ Cash Balance Plan
- ✓ DB(k)
- ✓ MyRA

Not only are there many to choose from, but these are only related to the types of retirement plan. Within these plans, there are a multitude of additional choices. If you own your own business, would you want to provide a matching contribution for your employees? You also have to decide which financial institution would you want to set up your plan?

If you are an employee of a company with a retirement, you also have to decide how much you are going to contribute each week, which investments you are going to invest in, and who your beneficiary will be. Once you decide all of this, then you have to fill out the paperwork. With so many choices it can seem virtually impossible to choose the right one. Just reading about all of the choices makes your head hurt.

The problem isn't made any easier by the fact that there are many different people who are going to share contradictory opinions. Eventually, you become so overloaded with choices that the easiest thing to do is not make any decision at all. Naturally, that's exactly what most people opt for.

In a 2004 work titled *Asset Allocation and Information Overload: The Influence of Information Display, Asset Choice, and Investor Experience*, authors Julie Agnew and Lisa R. Szykman at the Boston College Center for Retirement Research studied this exact problem. To do so, they compared two groups of individuals, one with little financial knowledge and the other with a better understanding of personal finance.

As part of their study, they analyzed the tendency of test subjects in both groups to give up when presented with too many choices. Specifically, they found that those with lesser financial knowledge were overwhelmed when they had fewer than six different choices. When more than that were introduced, even the knowledgeable individuals started to experience decision fatigue. Is it any wonder, then, that most of us have trouble taking action when presented with nearly a dozen types of retirement accounts to choose from… and a virtually endless list of financial products to fill them with?

Not long ago, a financial advisor I know told me the story of a man he tried to work with. We'll call him Brian. Brian came to the financial advisor as a wealthy small business owner. He had a 401(k) through his company, but was looking for ways to save more money for a time when he would no longer be willing or able to work. He asked my friend which retirement plan would be best. The advisor created a proposal that showed him which option matched his situation, and why. Unfortunately, Brian decided not to act on the information at the time.

After a year had passed, the financial advisor got another call from Brian. As it turned out, his business was still running strong, but Brian wasn't making any headway on additional contributions to his retirement. Did my friend remember him, Brian wondered, and would he be able to help? The advisor assured Brian that he remembered him, and reiterated that he would be pleased to assist in any way he could.

At this point, Brian mentioned that he was revisiting his retirement plan again and wanted to know how he could save more money for the future. Wanting his potential client to get on track, the advisor recommended a personal meeting in his office. The two got together and had a long talk about the type of retirement plan that would best meet Brian's goals. The advisor felt he had laid out the perfect strategy for the business owner to follow. However, Brian once again wanted to go home and think about it.

Nothing more happened until Brian called the financial advisor again after another year. Once more he asked whether they could come up with a plan to save extra money for retirement. At this point, my friend remarked that he was starting to feel like Bill Murray in the movie *Groundhog Day*, reliving the same conversation again and again.

The frustrating part about this story isn't that Brian asked the same questions again and again – it's that he didn't get started when he had the opportunity. Had Brian just put away $500 per month for those first three years and chosen an average investment option earning seven percent per year, those initial savings could have grown to more than $100,000 25 years later, even if he hadn't done anything else. Instead, because he hesitated, his chances of enjoying a comfortable retirement got a little worse.

There are millions of us like Brian around the country. We have the money to save, if only we are willing to set it aside and make our retirement a priority. But we get overwhelmed by the choices and caught up in the fine print, so never truly moving forward as a result.

> *Understand that you probably aren't going to make perfect decisions when it comes to your finances. But anything you can start with today is significantly better than doing nothing.*

Over the last 30 years, Congress has tried to address our lack of savings by creating new plans that are supposed to be simple and easy to maintain. Now there are so many of them, each with its own set of rules, that it's more difficult than ever to make a smart decision. But if you can simply choose a retirement account that's likely to work for you, other changes fall in line and the effects start to snowball.

None of this starts, however, until you make an initial decision. It's easy to be afraid of making the wrong choice, which can prevent you from taking any action at all. Or, you can simply choose what works (or you think works) for someone else. If you ask around about retirement savings and you'll hear things like:

"My brother-in-law handles our retirement. He's a CPA!"

"I asked my neighbor what type of plan he has. I figured he must know what is doing."

"I read an article that said all business owners should have this type of retirement plan…"

Make no mistake: There isn't a shortage of financial information and you won't go lacking for opinions either. There are plenty of people out there who will gladly tell you that you should opt for an IRA, a Roth

IRA, a regular 401(k), or something else. Unfortunately, just because they have a some knowledge about what's worked for them, or a background in one area of finance, that doesn't mean they have the answers to your retirement questions and challenges.

It's fine to listen to others and get their input. Never forget that you have to be the one to decide what fits your situation best, though. **When we let others make choices for us, that we are too busy to make ourselves, we are giving away our power to create the retirement we dream of.**

All too often you will hear people say, "there isn't enough time in the day." When you believe that there isn't enough time in the day to create a retirement plan, you have made a choice; the choice of in-action. The choice to do nothing is caused by the fact that we have too many choices. We make choices every day, and the choices we make help shape our world.

Dave Farrow is the 2 Time Guinness World Record Holder, for memorizing and recalling the exact order of 59 decks of cards randomly shuffled together. That's 3,068 cards in total! This record was set to break his previous record of 52 decks of cards (see 1997 edition). This record is considered the most difficult memory feat in the Guinness Book of Records. During an interview on Yourmoneyshow.com Dave shocked the audience when he said that he was diagnosed with ADHD and Dyslexia at the age of 13. One would not think that someone who is ADHD or Dyslexic could have such a memory.

Dave's dad was a factory worker and basically told Dave he would only be able to become a blue collar worker. Dave's dad also told him that he would never be smart enough to be successful. Dave said during the interview that he became obsessed with proving his dad wrong. Dave wasn't willing to accept the choice of a being a blue collar worker like as his Dad. Dave decided to make a choice and become the world's greatest memory expert.

Like Dave, when you copy someone else's financial plan, adopt their beliefs, or make the same choices, you have given away your power. Once you have given away your ability to create the retirement you want, you are forced to accept whatever comes your way. Millions of seniors haven't saved for retirement or copied their neighbor's retirement plans.

Now they are facing a life of poverty wondering why me; what did I do to deserve this? The answer is that they gave away their power by failing to take the proper actions, such as educating themselves, following a strict budget, or paying off their debts. The more control you have, and the more involved you are, the better you're going to be able to create your own future.

There is an old saying that "a trip around the world begins with one step." Take that one step *today*. Put a few dollars in a savings account. Continue that every week and don't stop. From there, you can develop a habit that will bloom into more meaningful results. It will give you the confidence to participate in a 401(k), set up your own retirement accounts, and learn to invest. You don't have to do all of those things at once. If you don't get started, you have given away your power.

We all know that we are going to retire someday in the future, and that we need to save for that time. If you can make a handful of simple decisions now and start momentum working in your direction, then you'll be able to develop some patience and build up wealth over the long term. Put off those decisions, and you'll find yourself in a desperate attempt to amass wealth quickly. As you'll see, financial shortcuts hardly ever pan out.

# CHAPTER 6
## SHORTCUTS TAKE YOU NOWHERE FAST

The solution to the problem of saving for your retirement is incredibly obvious. After all, it's drummed into your consciousness on a daily basis by ads on television, the internet, and even magazines and newspapers, not to mention infomercials and get-rich-quick courses. This magic solution? *Shortcuts!*

For those who don't have the stamina and hunger for fame to live in the woods for months on end, there is an almost endless parade of materials that urge and offer other fast solutions. Consider just a few of the best-known books and products out there, many of which may already be familiar to you:

> *MONEY Master the Game: 7 Steps Financial Freedom* by Tony Robbins
> *The Road to Wealth* by Suzie Orman
> *The Total Money Makeover* by Dave Ramsey
> *The Automatic Millionaire* by David Bach
> *No Down Payment® Real Estate Techniques* taught by Carleton Sheets
> *Flip and Grow Rich* with Armando Montelongo
> *Fortune Builders* with Than Merrill
> *The 'Free and Clear' Tax Lien System* with John Beck

These are all well-known books and programs by respected experts. In many cases they contain important and useful information on accumulating wealth. At the same time they feed into the popular-held notion that large sums of money can be achieved quickly, almost *immediately*, with just a few basic steps. But as the saying goes, none of these programs works unless you do.

We live in a world where just about any skill in life is being presented as one you can master with a how-to book for "dummies." While it's true that most things aren't as complicated as they seem, the idea that you're going to solve your biggest financial challenges instantly is very likely to be mistaken.

No matter where you look there are new commercials and infomercials clogging up the airways. Day after day, these TV ads supposedly show "everyday people" who made fortunes in just a few short weeks; using straightforward techniques in stock trading, real estate, or some other business venture. They're careful to point out that you can buy the CD or videos and be on your way to instant wealth. Most of them even come with a 30-day money-back guarantee.

To judge by the advertising, everything you want in your life from better health to improved finances– can be obtained in a very short period of time; if you're just willing to spend the money and learn how. It doesn't matter if you don't have any particular skills or expertise. You don't even need to devote a lot of time. Just buy the next product and it's almost certain to happen for you.

The reality, as we all know, is that these claims tend to be overblown (at best). In fact, so many "financial experts" have been touting outlandish shortcuts that new rules have had to be put in place to curb the lies. In 2008, the Federal Trade Commission act was passed to prevent advertisers from making wild claims that can't be proven. That's why you see so many small-print disclaimers on the ads you come across.

While the spokesperson claims that applicants can be given a credit line in as little as two months, the disclaimer quietly points out that "most customers should expect to receive a credit line within 8 to 12 months." An infomercial that touts a proven method of earning up to $1,000 per week, is legally required to be followed by a short correction that notes "most members don't earn $1,000 per week. Most customers earn approximately $100 per week."

Advertisers don't really want you paying attention to the fine print, and millions of customers will happily oblige. Despite the warnings, most of us are willing to buy that infomercial product in hopes that this will be "the one". How many times have you spent money on one of these programs and how many times have they worked out? Despite the offers that make everything sound so good and easy, they rarely ever deliver what they promise.

That isn't to say that there isn't good information on financial planning, real estate, and other topics out there. There absolutely is – it's just that most of it is already available for free, online and at your library. Most people just don't want to spend the effort learning it the hard way.

So, let me tell you the secret about so-called secrets: There are no shortcuts to saving for retirement. However, that's not the bad news you might think it is. The process of planning for a successful financial future doesn't have to be agonizing, frustrating, or time-consuming. It doesn't involve an excessive amount of work. In fact, the principles have remained unchanged for decades: Buy low, sell high, and keep at it. The formula for a comfortable retirement is to make more, spend less, and save what you can.

The fact of the matter is that if there were simple, quick, easy tips or strategies that you can use to become wealthy, all of us would be rich. The shortcuts were always imaginary and anyone who makes things sound easier than they are, is probably trying to take their own shortcut at your expense. Anything and everything worth doing in this life takes time and effort.

Some of us are going to have it easier than others. If you are in your 20s or 30s, then it's going to be easier for you to start saving with relatively small amounts and see dramatic results over time. If you're in your 50s, on the other hand, then time is of the essence. But even knowing that, the worst thing you can do is to risk what you have in hopes of a quick return. You could end up losing it all and then start from an even worse position than you're currently in.

Remember that if something sounds too good to be true, then it probably is. There are multiple investment and savings options that can provide income and growth, if you are willing to spend the time to educate yourself. You don't have to be a professional advisor or a "shark" with millions to burn. Instead, you just have to take a more than casual interest in your retirement fund and financial future.

Take a step back and look at some of the people our society considers to be "successful." Then, ask yourself what kind of work they put in to reach that point. Would you ever imagine that LeBron James practiced basketball 20 minutes a day, three times a week before becoming a superstar? Would you believe it if someone told you Tiger Woods mastered his golf game in a few hours practicing Monday through Friday? Could Derek Jeter have become a fourteen-time All-Star and five-time Golden Glove winner for the Yankees by taking a course and then putting in 15 minutes each morning?

We know each of these things would've been impossible. After all, in order to win fourteen major championships, Tiger Woods practices from seven hours a day or more. So why would we believe we can be the best at something if we are only willing to put in a minimal amount of effort? It just doesn't add up.

Advertisers want you to believe that all you have to do to achieve your wildest dreams is follow someone else's step-by-step instructions for a few minutes when you have free time. That's a far cry from the lessons of our parents, grandparents, teachers, and coaches who instilled in us that practice makes perfect.

Shortcuts fail because the authors and gurus who present them to you skip the most important step. By glancing over the difficult work it takes to make it to the top, they are essentially showing you a blueprint to build your dream home without providing the hammer, nails, and wood you will need to build it.

There is a truth you have to accept before we can go further: **You** can change your future without shortcuts. You *can* achieve and create your retirement. You might face some obstacles on the path to financial freedom, but we can show you how to address them.

Most of us have incurred some financial obstacle at one point or another. It could have been the loss of a job, a serious illness, an accident involving a car or home, or even a bankruptcy. After such a setback it's common to believe that we have lost or have been defeated.

The most powerful changes in your life will come from you and your ability and willingness to shift your own perspective. Altering your thoughts and beliefs about saving is far more important than the specific investment strategies.

Real improvement begins in your mind and then manifests itself in your behavior and the world around you. For that reason, adjusting your mindset and your beliefs is more important to your retirement plans than changing what it says on your bank statements.

# CHAPTER 7
## THE ZERO SUM GAME

There is a myth that most of us have been duped into believing. It's called the "zero sum game," and it may have impacted your way of thinking, investing, and believing. It represents the theory that if you are in competition with someone for anything in life, only one of you can win. It states that if you win, your competition loses; and if your competition wins, then you have to lose.

The unfortunate thing about the zero sum game is that it doesn't account for a win-win outcome. Nor does it recognize that many times, "losing" drives the loser to win later. In a zero sum mindset, losing is instant and permanent. In the real world, though, we usually find success when we take a bigger view of what winning actually means in the long run.

Let's look at an example of what I'm talking about. The Famous Amos brand was started by Wally "Famous" Amos himself, who had a knack for making and selling cookies. Eventually, he built up a large and successful business around his products and image. After some time, though, Wally sold the majority of his thriving cookie company to a third party, along with his branding rights. It seemed like a great deal for everyone involved. Famous Amos was (and still is) a name that people recognized and associated with great taste.

At some time after he had become a minority owner in the company he started, Wally decided to stop by the plant where his cookies were being produced. The new owners had changed the recipes to boost profits, and the new batches didn't measure up to his standards of quality. Following a disagreement, Wally agreed to sell the remainder of his stake to the other partners – he didn't want to be in the business of selling the ordinary.

With that move, Wally was officially out of the cookie business. Even worse, he lost the branding rights to his own name, so he couldn't turn around and build up another cookie company from scratch. If he had subscribed to a zero sum belief, it would have been easy for him to feel like he had lost everything and would struggle to find a new business venture. Instead, as he once told a radio audience on YourMoneyShow.com, the setback motivated him to try something new. "I did it once," Wally told listeners, "and I knew I could do it again."

Rather than accept defeat, Wally decided that his grandmother's muffin recipe would make money. It did. Today Uncle Wally's sells muffins in more than 10,000 stores nationwide and is a multimillion-dollar enterprise. He's proof that the zero sum game exists in our minds, not in the real world.

Despite the fact that thousands of stories like this one play out every day, in our society we generally act as if there is only one winner in any situation. Just turn on the TV, or visit your favorite website, and you'll see the victors of a sporting event or reality TV show being talked about in the media. Ask yourself: Do you remember who *lost* the Super Bowl or World Series in the last few years? You might if your favorite team was the loser. Most people, however, will only remember who won.

This concept of win-or-lose thinking and being the best has also crept into our everyday lives. When neighbors talk, it's generally not about one who drives an older car and seems to be getting by just fine. Instead, we notice the neighbor who drives a brand-new Tesla, or the one who recently renovated their house to make it look like a mansion.

Rob Fore offers another example of what's possible when we reject zero sum thinking. In the early '90s, he had a dental supply business. Unfortunately, he made a very poor business decision and was forced to file for bankruptcy within a few months as a result. He lost his home to foreclosure not long after. His wife and son went to live with his mother-in-law.

Rob chose not to move in with his mother-in-law along with the rest of his family. Instead, he slept on a urine-stained mattress he found on the side of the road. Although he could have moved in with family, he was too proud to do so. More than that, he wanted to take personal responsibility for his bad choices. Rob wanted to live with the consequences, and feel them, so he could motivate himself to be better in the future.

How many people have you ever met who would even *consider* owning up to their own mistakes like that? Rob faced up to his mistake, continued to work, and eventually made enough money to buy a home and moved back with his wife and son. You might think that would be the logical end to the story, but he continued to live outdoors for several more months.

Rather than turn back to comfort, Rob chose to be homeless to prove to himself that he could survive it. If he could make it through the day eating out of trash cans and living outside, he knew he could survive anything. He did something most of us wouldn't dream of, choosing to remain on the streets for more than six months while he got his life back together.

Rob didn't buy into the zero sum game. He knew that his setbacks were temporary, and that other opportunities were coming his way. He felt in his core that it was only a matter of time before he, too, would achieve success. He never believed that he had lost or been defeated. Instead, he held tight to the conviction that he would one day be successful – and now he is, as a millionaire several times over in the multilevel marketing industry.

Do you believe in a zero sum world? Is that idea holding you back, consciously or unconsciously? There is a prevailing attitude that tells us it is difficult to save and invest money. Moreover, there is a widespread acceptance of the view that there is a limited amount of money in the world, and that it's increasingly making its way to the top one percent in our country. And so, when we view the number of jobs available to us, or the amount of money the population can have at its disposal, we tend to think in finite amounts.

As Gary notes extensively in his first book *It Was YOU, All Along* most people talk about getting a "piece of the pie" as if the size of the pie were constant and never changing. If you internalize that belief, then you may feel like you have to do anything possible to get the biggest slice possible. But as with all things related to zero sum thinking, focusing on imagined scarcity causes you to miss the bigger picture.

This is easy to see if we take a larger view of the economy. Although the top one percent *have* seen their wealth increase significantly over the last 10 years, that's not the end of the story. There were 142.3 million people employed in non-military jobs in December 2005. Of course, the financial crisis and recession slowed the country down, dropping employment to 139 million in November 2010. Many men and women took note of this, and assumed that things have gotten worse than ever over the last decade. The numbers say differently. There were 149.9 million people employed as of December 2015. That represents an increase of almost 11 million jobs since 2010, and 7.6 million more than there were 10 years ago *before* the crisis.

We have more people working now than we did in the past. In fact, there are *substantially* more jobs available. There are numerous opportunities out there for people to earn an income and increase their overall wealth. The recession was a momentary downturn, not an ending point.

Additionally, surveys show the number of millionaires in our country has risen. A recent CNBC article (backed by research from Spectrem Group) found that there were 10.1 million households in the U.S. with $1 million or more in investable assets, not counting the value of their primary residence. That figure is up from 9.6 million in 2013, and also tops the pre-recession peak of 9.2 million in 2007. In fact, it's the highest number recorded since Spectrem began tracking the data in 1997. Could it really be impossible to create wealth in the U.S. at a time when *millions* of us are doing it?

In case you're curious, the number of households worth $5 million or more also set a new record, jumping from 1.24 million in 2013 to 1.3 million now. And, there are now 142,000 households worth $25 million or more, up from 132,000 in 2013. While it's fair to say the rich are getting richer, what is more notable is that increasing numbers of Americans are becoming wealthy. The U.S. has gained or added back more than 3.5 million millionaires since the financial crisis. There are now twice as many as there were in 1996.

Those figures don't support the zero sum mindset, but they *do* reinforce what we already know about the power of patience. One detail that emerged in these surveys on wealth was that the average age among millionaires was 62, suggesting that most had built up their nest eggs over a lifetime. Among those worth $25 million or more, the average age was 65, but the majority were still working. One in 5 owned or started their own companies, and seventy percent worked more than 40 hours per week. A full two-thirds were part of dual-income households.

The financial pie isn't fixed. Its size keeps growing. There's plenty of room and opportunity for you to enjoy a comfortable retirement if you begin saving *today*.

The zero sum game is a myth. Defeat is never final unless you give up. Most of us have incurred some kind of financial setback at one point or another. It could have been the loss of a job, a serious illness, an accident involving a car or home, or even a bankruptcy. While each of these can feel like the end of the line as far as retirement saving plans go, the reality is that there are countless others who have lived through the same thing and come back stronger.

Even some of the best-known and most accomplished individuals suffered major setbacks and failures. What separated them from everyone else was their determination to learn from them and keep moving forward. Steve Jobs – hailed as the innovator and business genius behind Apple – once launched a home computer named Lisa that fell flat. Oprah Winfrey was fired from her first job in broadcasting. Michael Jordan was cut from his high school basketball team, and Sylvester Stallone was so broke and homeless before his Hollywood breakthrough that he had to sell his dog (he later bought it back at a substantial markup).

You can achieve your retirement and savings goals by changing your perception of what is possible, and what it means to suffer a setback. Decide today that you're going to think in terms of detours and speed bumps, not failures that cause you to give up. The zero sum mindset only applies to you if you let it.

If you can change your perception, though, everything else in your life will change along with it.

# CHAPTER 8
## CHANGE YOUR PERCEPTION, CHANGE YOUR WORLD

If you are like most Americans living today, you might expect to have a 40-year working career – for example, starting your first "real," non-entry-level job at the age of 30 and retiring at the age of 70. If you were to average $50,000 per year in pay over that time, you would earn $2 million. Obviously, you'll have to pay bills and taxes, so you wouldn't ever see much of that money, much less save it. However, imagine for a moment that you could spend *half* of your income on those necessities and stuff the rest under your mattress. When it came time to retire, you would have $1 million in cold hard cash… even without any interest or appreciation.

So, are you on track to have $1 million at retirement? Probably not. The question, then, is why won't you have more to show for your four decades of work? There are only two possible answers: Either you don't believe you can save that much money, or you feel that spending your earnings today is more important than having access to them later.

While it's true that housing, insurance, food, transportation, and health care are taking a bigger bite out of your paycheck, your belief has a much bigger effect on your rate of savings than the realities of budgeting do. If you believe that saving is a small priority in your life, you will predictably struggle to put aside money for your retirement every month.

When this happens, it's often because a person believes their financial situation to be outside of their control. They rationalize that the events in the world are more powerful than their own habits and let go of their responsibility to control their future. If you aren't doing a good enough job to prepare for the parts of your life that are yet to come, it isn't due to the unfortunate events you see in the news; it's all about the way you react to them. It might seem as if outside forces are being caused by someone else, or thrust upon you, but the fact of the matter is **you have helped to create them**.

Susan, a 60-year-old woman, was still working and had saved money in her 401(k). Like most seniors, she was having trouble paying her bills. She wanted to take a loan from her 401(k). When asked why she wanted the money she replied, "*It takes three paychecks to pay my rent, which is the cheapest I can find. I end up paying my rent every five weeks instead of each month. After a few months, I am behind again. With the fourth paycheck, I pay the car insurance, food, gas, phone, prescriptions, medical and utilities. There is not even enough money to cover all my expenses. Although I don't have credit card bills, sometimes I have to decide between paying for my blood pressure medication and buying food. To add insult to injury, my molar is cracked and I am in need of a root canal, which I will not be able to afford.*"

For some people, they aren't spending money, they just don't have it. Many people, like Susan, are doing all they can, yet are facing the overwhelming costs of basic living expenses, including medicine. For many other, their expenses are more than their income. Regardless of whether your expenses are more than you make, have bad credit, are without savings, or are carrying large credit card balances, consider that YOU contributed to the difficult circumstances you are facing. Some might object to this, saying "Why would I want to create a bad situation that will have a negative impact on my life?" The answer is that you didn't do so consciously, but you did it all the same.

We all like to daydream and let our imaginations run wild. What we often fail to remember that our actions are inevitably powered by our beliefs. That is, what we think we bring about. What we believe tends to manifest itself in reality.

Let's use a real-world example. Suppose you have a bad day at work. Maybe you start to imagine better times ahead. Perhaps you even begin to consider what it would be like to work closer to home, spend fewer hours at the office, and not have to deal with your demanding boss. These images comfort you, so you start to go over them in your mind again and again. Slowly but subtly, you reinforce the idea that you would be better off without your current job in an emotional way.

In your conscious mind you are simply watching a movie or playing out a fantasy. However, your brain doesn't know the difference between that far-off notion and the reality of your need for employment. As a result, you begin to subconsciously act on these dreams. You start to show up a little bit later each morning, forget important tasks, and let your performance decline. The gradual result is that you are terminated from your job, which allows your mind to reach its goal of letting you look for work closer to home, and to find a boss who will treat you better. After all, wasn't that the image you fed it repeatedly?

When things are going your way, it's not difficult to understand that everything happens for a reason, or that we are responsible for our own destiny. But when you're getting fired, or dealing with difficult financial circumstances, it's much harder to face up to this fact. When things don't go as planned, it's much simpler to simply assume that the world is out to get you.

In those moments, there is something I want you to remember:

> ***There are universal laws to life that are incredibly consistent. No universal law applies only part of the time.***

> *In fact, universal laws either apply always or none of the time; there is no in-between scenario.*

If you created the circumstances that led to getting a great job and being promoted within a company, then you must have *also* created all the events that led up to your termination. No one is doing anything to you. There is no "negative force" out there somewhere causing bad things to happen to you. No life force is acting upon you or holding you back. You created each outcome with your own thoughts and beliefs.

Understanding that we are all setting the direction for our own lives isn't just the cornerstone of this book, but also for planning a successful future (financial and otherwise). Until you embrace it, there is very little you can change or improve about your situation. So, how can we use this realization to help save for a comfortable retirement? We can begin by looking at the tools that are available to us in a different way.

For many people, the legislation that brought about IRAs and 401(k)s could be considered as failures. Statistically speaking, they haven't provided Americans with the retirement income they need. According to The Economic Policy Institute's *State of the American Retirement*, these tools account for less than three percent of seniors' total income, even though they should represent a big chunk of savings by now. Even Ted Benna, considered by many to be the father of the 401(k), has stated he is not a fan of what he began. In interviews, he has repeatedly stated that his preference would be to scrap the whole system and start over.

Yet, there is significant value to having a 401(k). Your parents probably retired because they received a traditional pension plan as part of their post-career income package. Those pension systems weren't replaced overnight, but gradually over time. This trend wasn't secret, and anyone could have taken notice of it. If you didn't, then where have you been? Why have you not taken responsibility for your own financial security already?

If your 401(k) isn't large enough to meet your retirement needs, is that really the fault of "the system"? Did the government or business world somehow fail you? Of course not. Saying that 401(k)s don't work is like saying the math test was too hard even though you didn't study for it. If you haven't saved enough for retirement, then it's not fair to blame the tools available; the shortcoming has to do with your failure to understand the options that are out there and make proper use of them. Remember, a janitor and gas station attendant was able to save $8 million. The odds are *not* stacked against your success.

Gary has accumulated the bulk of his savings via 401(k) plans from each company where he worked in the past. Both he and his wife invested money into their accounts consistently, learning to "pay themselves first" by funding their retirement plans and then learning to live off of what was left in their paychecks. Only then did they take out money for standard living expenses.

Most people take an opposite approach, spending all of their money and then wondering why there isn't anything left for retirement. They certainly don't use all of the tools that are available to them. For example, most employers use a 401(k) plan that matches a portion of your salary or contribution. However, according to a 2014 study by Aon Hewitt, 26.9% of 401(k) participants – more than a quarter – do not contribute a large enough percentage to receive their full employer match. They are throwing away money that could be theirs. This is such an epidemic that the Financial Industry Regulatory Authority (FINRA) actually issued an alert on their website[2] to educate workers and let them know that they are losing out on these savings.

---

2 *http://www.finra.org/investors/alerts/why-leave-money-make-most-employers-401k-match*

What are these employees getting for their money that's worth more than a secure future? According to the *2015 Retirement Confidence Survey* by Employee Benefit Research Institute, twenty-four percent of respondents noted they wouldn't need to give up *anything* to save up an extra $25 per week. Twelve percent thought they would have to stop going to the movies or downloading films online to come up with the same amount. Eleven percent admitted they would need to give up expensive coffee, and eight percent would be forced to stop buying lottery tickets.

To be fair, there *are* people who simply can't afford to contribute more to their retirement right now. However, most just don't want to, since it would mean eliminating another purchase that gives them instant gratification. We all want to feel good now. Shopping, going out to dinner, and spending money on vacations all provide an immediate boost. Saving for the future doesn't bring this gratification we are all looking for. It is difficult for all of us to focus on what we will require 20-40 years from now. Yet, doing so is vital. But if your future self could come back and tell you one thing, most likely it would be to begin saving now.

You weren't born with a retirement nest egg, but you weren't born with loads of debt or a poor credit score, either. The system didn't fail you and no one is out to get you. All of this happened because of what you believe and the decisions you have made along the way.

That starts with you believing that you can save more. You need to take the time today to find out which options are available to you and see how you can take advantage of them. You may discover that your retirement account could be growing much faster if you would only add a few more dollars a month and let the company you work for contribute more, too.

Whether you like it or not, your attitudes and beliefs have a significant impact on the reality you create for yourself. This isn't just a self-help mantra; it's the truth about the way you shape your future. Most people end up in the same types of jobs and personal relationships again and again.

As Dr. Phil likes to tell his guests, in each circumstance in your life, "you are the common denominator." You have created the opportunities you received, and the challenges that have gotten in your way. If your savings aren't sufficient, it's due to the choices you have made. It's not the case that you can't catch a break – when it comes to retirement planning, things don't happen *to* you... they happen *because* of you.

If you feel like you're stuck in a rut with regard to your bills, expenses, and savings, you may have created your self-repeating cycle. It works like this:

> ***You create your experiences based on your beliefs. Your beliefs lead to similar subsequent experiences, which cause you to reinforce the same belief. Unless you change your beliefs, your actions will remain the same and you will create the same experiences all over again.***

Let's take a look at one of these cycles in day-to-day life. Suppose for a moment that you always seem to pay your bills late, and for that reason are always paying late fees. You're constantly running behind financially and feel like you never have enough money. You get the sense that "there is too much month left at the end of a paycheck," so to speak. Consequently, every time you think about paying a bill, you have those feelings of not having enough money. You get a sense, emotionally, of lacking income and wealth.

These thoughts will carry over to other parts of your life. When you see a new car, you'll be reminded of one other thing you can't afford. The same might happen when it comes to smaller everyday items, like clothing, home repairs, or items for your family. The more you live paycheck to paycheck, the more deeply ingrained into this rut you become. Eventually, every situation becomes a reminder that you don't have enough income or wealth to get ahead.

Regardless of whatever started this cycle, you get in the habit of not paying your bills on time and those feelings become stronger and stronger. After a long hard day at work, and driving the kids around to their after-school activities, making them dinner, and helping them with their homework, you finally find a few minutes to yourself. The last thing you're going to want to do at that moment is take on an activity that reminds you of your current economic situation. So you pay less attention to the bills and the cycle is further reinforced.

None of this will change until your feelings and beliefs about your income and situation are replaced. Unless that happens, you will create the same experience over and over. Before you can alter your situation, you have to improve your attitude about it so your actions can start to move in a new direction.

"How can I simply turn off a deeply held belief?" you might ask. "Isn't that impossible?" It certainly is not. But to do so, you have to examine whether the belief is actually true, and figure out what you gain by holding on to it. For instance, you probably don't hate paying *all* bills. Most people would consider the act of paying off a credit card, sending in the last check for an auto loan, or mailing a final mortgage payment to be deeply satisfying. Why couldn't you feel that way about the rest of your bills, or the payments that come in between?

When you pay your bills on time, you save money. Likewise, when you send your hard-earned cash to the utilities company, or pay your rent, you are doing things that are reasonable, acceptable, and good for your well-being. So, the issue isn't paying the money; it's your *perception* of the bill that's the problem.

To see how perspective alters your impressions, imagine you were planning to head out for a picnic in the park, or possibly a round of golf. Perhaps these activities were going to be the highlight of your weekend after a particularly grueling workweek. If you were just about to leave the house and it started to rain, you might feel very frustrated and disappointed.

Now imagine a hot summer day where you have spent the whole day planting flowers and mowing the lawn. In this scenario, you might be pleased to see a bit of afternoon rain to cool you off and give your flowers some water. In either situation, the external event is constant – water falls from the sky just like it does many times per year. You are not angry that it is raining. You're angry because the rain changed the outcome you desired.

You have to hold on to the right beliefs about money. If you want to create a mindset of prosperity, you need to be consistent in your beliefs and actions. Remember what we told you before: **Universal laws are constant. Your beliefs will influence you again and again.**

Many of us have very strong beliefs about our families. If you are a parent, you likely feel that you want to do anything you can to care for your children. You would never consider doing something that would cause them unnecessary harm or discomfort. Hence, your actions are always consistent. Your beliefs about your loved ones guide you in day-to-day life so that you always prioritize your kids.

You could apply that mindset to saving for your future. When it comes down to it, putting money away for your retirement is all about caring for yourself and your family. In addition, it is about believing that you have value, deserve to have the money you need to live comfortably when you retire, and don't want to become dependent on anyone (especially your children). Paying your bills on time, and ensuring you save a portion of your earnings, is a way of adding value for your family and creating opportunities for a better tomorrow.

Simply changing the way you think about money in this way could alter your habits in a big way. The effects of consistency flow through everything in your life. You can't be dishonest and unethical at work while remaining a saint in your home life. Nor can you make your health a priority during the day and then ignore it by drinking, smoking, or eating unhealthy foods in the evening. You can attempt to, or believe you can strike a balance, but sooner or later the two forces will contradict each other and create massive problems. You either believe in something or you don't.

Abundance is a state of mind, not a financial condition. If you believe you can have abundance now, you will also believe you can have it in the future when you retire. If you are struggling to save money, you can't assume you aren't going to feel poor in the future. Just as a mindset of wealth builds wealth, concentrating on poverty attracts more poverty.

We mean this in a literal sense. If you feel poor, you *will* attract poverty. To see this phenomenon in action, consider that many of the people who win the lottery, lose all of their money within a few years. Usually, it's because they have invested poorly, or spent lavishly without taking the time to look after their finances. How could they manage to go broke after being gifted millions? It's easy to understand when you realize that both abundance and poverty are states of mind and belief. People that obtain wealth and lose it often do not have an abundance consciousness – a mental image of themselves being comfortable with money. Hence, despite having financial resources for short time, these people *feel* poor and consequently end up back where they were.

The poverty mindset often originates from a low sense of self-esteem. Someone who is gifted a large sum of money, but subconsciously feels that they don't deserve it, will find a way to lose it. Strange as it might sound, they were mentally and emotionally uncomfortable with having a lifestyle they felt was beyond their reach.

Abundance, on the other hand, isn't only about material wealth. It also relates to health, knowledge, time, friends, happiness, security, compassion, and all the other good things that come in life. If you are outside looking at the trees, hearing the birds, and enjoy the feeling of the sun shining on your face, you might feel like you don't have a care in the world. Conversely, if you feel as if you're constantly rushed and are always running late, you will be disorganized. The difference, once again, is a matter of perspective. Everyone has the same 24 hours in a day, yet you can feel abundant in your schedule or impoverished by the hours and minutes you're sure you don't have.

If you are not doing a good job of saving money now, there is a good chance that the lack of saving is representative of how you view yourself and your situation. With a growing family, it's easy to have your paycheck split in many directions. Much of it will have to go toward rent or mortgage, car payments, food, clothing, insurance and medical bills, and even savings for college. But at the same time, contributing to your 401(k) or IRA every week is a consistent action that shows you care about yourself and your loved ones. You believe that having enough money to live on, comfortably throughout your golden years, is very important.

The first step to breaking a repeating cycle is recognizing that a lack of saving is not the fault of society, the markets, or any other external force. Instead, it's a product of your belief. If you believe you don't have enough money, or don't deserve to be wealthy, then ask yourself what you are gaining from those beliefs? The answer is nothing. That belief is holding you back. If you can recognize that stumbling block for what it is, you'll be able to find a way to change your future beliefs and experiences.

As difficult as it might be to accept when some of our plans are going poorly, we really do create our own world. We build it every day, on a decision-by-decision basis. It's easy to lose track of the power we have over ourselves, or attitudes, and our future. Once we begin to perceive the world around us differently, we can take the next step and start to create one that reflects our true desires.

Real change starts with facing up to the one universal truth that matters: ***It was you, all along***.

# CHAPTER 9
## IT WAS YOU

In the last chapter, we pointed out a truth that is both uncomfortable and liberating at the same time: **that nothing happens *to* you; it happens *because* of you and what you believe.** Your savings and investment results don't come down to what others are doing, what's happening with the economy and stock market, or what your employer has or hasn't made available. Your beliefs and decisions have led you to this point.

Émile Coué was a French psychologist and pharmacist who did extensive research in the area of belief. To prove a point about the way perception can affect outcomes, Coué had subjects imagine they had placed a piece of wood 12 inches wide on the floor. Each person he asked said they would be able to walk from one end of the board to the other without any problems. Coué then had them imagine the same piece of wood, but suspended between two buildings 30 stories high. He discovered that just *thinking* about being on a piece of wood that far off the ground could make people shake and tremble. The question is why?

When the board is on the floor, you believe you can walk from one end of the other without getting hurt. When the same board is suspended in the air, though, you believe you will fall off. Once that belief takes hold, it becomes nearly impossible for you to make the short journey from one side to the other.

Even if you aren't aware of it, you probably have many similar beliefs that make it nearly impossible to save. Some of the most common mindsets related to retirement and savings are:

- ✓ "I'll never have enough money to retire."
- ✓ "I don't make enough money to retire, and never will."
- ✓ "Investing in the stock market is like gambling."
- ✓ "I can't save money because I live paycheck to paycheck."
- ✓ "All annuities are bad investments."
- ✓ "I'm not knowledgeable in finances, and learning about investing is too hard."
- ✓ "A 401(k) and company match are not as helpful for saving today as they were 10 years ago."

The list could go on and on. You could fill an entirely new book with a list of negative beliefs that people have and hold on to. Whether you like it or not, if you share some of these beliefs, they are going to have a significant impact on the reality you are creating for yourself. They will keep you from finding success and stability. You create your financial future by choosing what you believe in today. You can't alter the world around you; you can only transform yourself and your attitudes. Strangely enough, however, what you'll discover is that when you change your own beliefs, your surroundings and circumstances will adapt themselves to you.

Most of the people reading these pages will have heard this advice before, but might not have accepted it. To show you how powerful it is, I want to share another example of a real-life person who put these principles into action. His name is Dōv Baron, and he is the best-selling author of several books, including the recent *Fiercely Loyal: How High-Performing Companies Develop and Retain Top Talent*. You may have seen Dōv on TV or read some of his work. He's been featured by *CNN, USA*

*Today, Entrepreneur, CBS Small Business Pulse, SHRM, Yahoo Finance, Boston Globe, CEO Magazine,* and many other media outlets.

What makes Dōv especially relevant to the subject at hand isn't his business expertise, however, but an event from his personal life. In the summer of 1990, he decided to go free climbing after a rainstorm. If you aren't familiar with the sport, it involves scaling a mountain or cliff without any ropes, harnesses, or other protective equipment. You simply get to the top relying on your own ability.

While it was a pleasant sunny day, the stones and ground were still slippery from the rain that had fallen earlier. Dōv decided to climb anyway, getting about 11 stories high before he reached for a rock that dislodged and sent him hurling down onto the jagged earth below. Unconscious, he fell from the 120-foot cliff at roughly 70 mph. The impact of his collision with the ground shattered most of the bone structure of his face, disintegrating parts of his upper jaw and fracturing his lower jaw in four different places. Dōv also suffered a broken neck, four cracked ribs, and fractured bones in his leg and clavicle.

As if that weren't unfortunate enough, he had fallen into a valley where rescue workers couldn't get to him. With his body broken in a dozen places, and blood pouring into his boots, Dōv walked up the mountain to an open area where rescue workers could transport him to a nearby rural hospital. The grueling march, which would normally have lasted 45 minutes, took him three hours to complete.

Once he arrived at the hospital, doctors X-rayed Dōv's body and determined he was too badly injured for them to assist. As a small regional facility, they didn't have the equipment to tend to his wounds, and needed to transport him to a bigger medical center one hour away.

If the initial injuries hadn't killed most climbers, the delays in treatment might have. But, Dōv is anything but a normal free climber. In addition to being an outdoor enthusiast and media personality, he is known as Dr. Dōv Baron, a quantum meta-psychologist who spent 20 years meeting, studying, and living with mental and spiritual masters from a variety of disciplines and philosophies. His interests ranged from ancient Jewish Mysticism to Gnostic Christianity, Vendatic Hinduism, Buddhist philosophy, and the teachings of miracles.

Each of these backgrounds gave Dōv a deeper insight into the laws of manifestation, and the ways quantum physics, metaphysics, and psychology come together. He knew most people aren't using the full potential of their own minds.

While being transported to the city hospital, Dōv used his knowledge of the mind to heal himself. By the time the second set of doctors was able to review him, X-rays showed that he had no broken bones from the neck down. Was this a miracle? Not in his mind. He states that if you know something to be true, then it will be true for you. Reality can be bent to your will.

The next time something truly jarring happens in your life, don't let it become a failure or a stopping point. It's possible you will lose your job, get divorced, find yourself with a low credit score, or wipe out your savings. If you accept that you created those events and allowed them to happen, you'll also be able to understand that reshaping your belief is the key to getting back on the right path. You are the only one who has the ability to shape your future, and to produce the experiences and environment you choose to live in. **It really *has* been you all along.**

This is not to say you won't ever get sick, you won't ever be poor, or that you can simply heal yourself just by thinking about it the way Dōv did. Changing your beliefs isn't just about positive thoughts; it also involves un-learning some of what you already believe to be true, and that's not an easy process. Just look at religious and political beliefs. People will fight with all their might – sometimes even to the death – to hold on to or defend their personal views. Very few of us are willing to walk back from a "truth" they have accepted, regardless of what it has or hasn't done for them. It is possible to change your beliefs, if you are willing to examine them and decide whether they should continue to influence your actions and decisions.

Not all experiences in your life are going to be pleasurable. You can't create a world that's free of problems and struggles. And that's a good thing. The fact of the matter is that you are here to learn from your mistakes and pick up lessons along the way. Sometimes, the only way you can get those lessons is by going through something difficult. There is no good without bad, no joy without pain, and no happiness without sadness. They are two sides of the same coin.

You don't have to go through a sad time to feel joy, but you'll understand and appreciate your happiness all the more for having lived through something difficult. Or to look at it in another way, you can obtain greater abundance when you understand why you had a lack of abundance in the first place.

Imagine for a moment that you are in your local supermarket doing your food shopping. After getting all of the things on your list, you get to the bread isle and discover that there is no bread. The store has not received their delivery of bread yet.

How would you feel? Angry? Upset? Annoyed? Probably one of the three, if not all of them. You have other errands that you must do and on top all of your errands, you must now go to another store just to get bread. You can't imagine that the store wouldn't have bread.

For people who lived during the Great Depression, this was their life. Food was scarce, many people were unemployed, and did not have any money even to buy food. So when families got a loaf of bread, they stretched it as far as they could.

For those who lived during the Great Depression, they understand poverty and not having access to basic essentials. Therefore, they are much better savers than their children as they appreciate their world and how fast they can obtain things by ordering online. However, they also appreciate where they came from and this is why many seniors today engage in the dangerous practice of pill splitting. To save money, many seniors split their pills in half. Unfortunately some pills can be split exactly in half. This results in varying dosages and can cause seniors to take more than the recommended dosage.

Today if something is broken, doesn't look right, or smell right we throw it away. There is so much that is available through the internet, places like Costco, or at the local supermarket that we don't think twice about replacing it. With all the abundance that we have grown up with, Baby Boomers and those part of Generation X, need to become better savers and adopt a savings attitude. We're not saying that you should become frugal, but the fact is that ***IT HAS BEEN YOU ALL ALONG***. You have the power to cut back on the excess in your life or spend all your savings so you can live today. You have the power to grow your wealth and abundance, by investing in yourself as you invest in your future. Within you is the ability to make your life and retirement into whatever you want them to be. The first step to building a better world around you is harnessing the energy of your thoughts, words, and actions.

Unfortunately, when it comes to finances, most people just don't think about the fact that they are in control. Some time back, Brett went to a local mall and interviewed people for his radio show. He asked the same question to everyone: "What is the maximum you can contribute to a 401(k)?" He got some very strange answers. The most common was "I don't know." Several individuals started off the interview by saying things like "You want to ask me questions about finances? You've got the wrong person…" More than a few said that their spouse handled the family finances.

These are great illustrations of what most people truly believe about money. These kinds of notions lead you to subconsciously sabotage your own results. No one wants to work their way into poverty, but it's easy to have happen if you fail to grasp the power of belief and how it shapes your reality on a day-to-day basis.

The story of Dõv's fall and subsequent healing of his broken bones is a great way to show the power of the mind, but it might seem far-fetched to you. So, I'd like to introduce an example that's a little bit closer to home. Just for a moment, stop and imagine the sound of nails on a chalkboard. Hear the awful screeching sound in your head as a teacher drags her sharp nails down in an effort to get the attention of her students. For many people, the mere description of this act is enough to send a shudder through their body and cause their face to scrunch up. That's an everyday example of the power of belief. The chalkboard isn't actually there, and neither is the teacher. But putting the thought in your imagination made it true for you, even if it didn't exist in the "real" world.

The same holds true even if you didn't shrink away at the idea of the chalkboard. In that case, your mind rejected the suggestion. It said to itself, subconsciously, "I don't see a chalkboard and I don't hear anything." That belief canceled out the one introduced.

Our beliefs are the most powerful force in the world. They drive our every thought and action. Take some time to step back and examine your attitudes about saving, and even about life in general.

Some of your beliefs may not hold up to scrutiny. For example, all parents want their children to be successful. Generally speaking, many believe that the only way for their offspring to find happiness and prosperity is to attend a good college. They further believe that getting into a good college requires a strong GPA, skillful tutors, and numerous SAT prep classes. These are all conventional assumptions that guide family decision-making every day. And yet, many in our country are rapidly learning that a college education doesn't fully prepare students for the next phase in their lives.

Consider the case of Anna Alaburda. It has been 10 years since she graduated from law school, but unfortunately she has yet to find a full-time position as an attorney despite the fact that she spent about $150,000 to acquire her degree. Now she's suing her alma mater, and she's far from alone. In the last several years, 15 different lawsuits have been filed by legal graduates who want to hold the schools that trained them accountable for a lack of employment opportunities upon graduation. While all this is going on, there are plumbers, carpenters, salespeople, and others all around them who are making a great living despite having far less education.

This is just an obvious example, but there are many others that illustrate the way our beliefs cause us to spend more than we need to. To keep up with the Joneses, you might drive a fancy car, go on exotic vacations, or buy the trendiest clothes. Why is that? Warren Buffett – at times the richest man in America – still lives modestly. You won't see him driving a luxury automobile, jetting to a South Pacific island, or dining at the fanciest restaurants. He can certainly afford to do so, but he doesn't. His belief system doesn't make it necessary for him to express himself in that manner.

Russell Conwell was the first motivational speaker in America, making presentations to audiences around the country well over 100 years ago. He is best remembered for one of his inspirational lectures, *Acres of Diamonds*, which was eventually published into a book. The story follows a man named Ali Hafed who was consumed by the desire to own jewels. He was so preoccupied with this pursuit that he sold his farm and left his family in search of riches. Unfortunately for Ali, he didn't find any. When his health deteriorated and he could no longer continue to look, he returned home to find his family was gone. Having nothing left, he committed suicide.

What made Ali's story particularly poignant was that the fellow who bought his farm discovered that it was built on top of one of the largest diamond mines ever discovered. They were literally a few feet from him the whole time, but he never saw them.

The point of the story Conwell told is that we often believe the grass is greener on the other side. We are convinced other people have what we want, whether it's a new phone, a new car, or something else. But those things never bring us the satisfaction we expect them to, and in fact often distract us from what's truly important.

Just like Ali, you already have everything you need to save for your retirement. The only thing missing is your belief in yourself and your abilities. If you do not believe in yourself, or respect yourself, why should anyone else give you *their* belief or respect? Your mindset can work for you or against you. Take the time to examine which of your assumptions is helping you through life, and which ones are holding you back.

Making these assessments is a good first step. The next one is to change your actions…

# CHAPTER 10
## YOUR ACTIONS SPEAK VOLUMES

At times, most of us have believed saving money is a problem for "later" and if any extra money is available from their paycheck, it can be used on something other than savings. We assume we will have enough time down the road to build up a retirement account that will sustain them through their golden years. With the figures and examples we've given, you are probably starting to realize that following those kinds of beliefs won't be good enough. There is an easy way to tell whether someone has the right beliefs about retirement, or anything else in their lives. You simply look at their behaviors.

If you were an Admiral in the Navy and you are attacking the enemy, would you only send one ship? Obviously not. The object is to win the war and you would use all the ships, planes and missiles you could get your hands on just to win. Yet this is not how most people save for retirement. Most people only have one IRA or 401k, or rather, not put an amount in a savings account once and then not add to it for years.

Your actions are directly linked to your beliefs, and they won't contradict those beliefs regardless of what you say to yourself and others. So, if we examine someone's bank account and see they're spending more money than they make, or burn through their disposable income on luxury items, we can't believe that their retirement is important to them regardless of what they may claim. Their actions convey their true beliefs about themselves and the world. Their words might express one thing, but the truth is always in their behaviors.

Marshall Sylver, is a world-renown hypnotist who has made it big. He has entertained audiences on The Late Show with David Letterman, Howard Stern, Rosie O'Donnell, Dr. Joy Browne, Donny & Marie, Sally Jesse Raphael, Montel Williams, and The Big Idea with Donny Deutsch, where he used the power of influence to have the host eat fire.

He didn't appear just once on these shows. He has appeared 5 times on the Howard Stern Show, The Late Show, and on The David Letterman Show. He is one of the most televised entertainers there is. Marshall wasn't born wealthy. He was homeless and lived in a station wagon with his ten siblings. He lived on a Michigan farm where his mother worked three jobs to support her children. As a child, he lived with such hardships as no running water, no electricity, and no telephone.

At the age of 16 he went to a hypnosis show. He was hypnotized to climb into the hypnotist's lap, stick his thumb in his mouth, and say, "Sing it again daddy". After the show he realized that hypnosis was pretty powerful and he learned everything he could about it. His actions were stating that he truly believed how powerful hypnosis was

At the time this book is written, California has been under a severe drought. Californians have cut back on their water usage and stopped watering their lawns. However, the severe drought didn't stop some of the richest celebrities from keeping their grass as green as possible. Celebrities have spoken up about being more eco-friendly. Yet many of them are using large amounts of water to keep their lawns green during the drought or travel in their gas guzzling vehicles. They may be telling people about their beliefs of being eco-friendlier, yet their actions of don't prove that they mean it.

Knowing that, what can we say about America's beliefs about saving? A 2014 Bank rate survey found that only thirty eight percent of

Americans would be able to cover a $1,000 emergency room visit, or meet an unexpected $500 auto repair expense. A similar survey conducted by Annamaria Lusardi of George Washington University, Peter Tufano of Oxford, and Daniel Schneider of Princeton asked individuals whether they could afford a $2,000 unexpected expense that would occur in the next month.

They found that more than a quarter could not, and roughly one in five could do so only if they pawned possessions or took out Payday loans. The fact that none of these people could draw on emergency savings when they needed, tells us everything about their beliefs. They believe that spending is more important than saving it.

It's worth pointing out that the reverse is true on a subconscious level. If you aren't saving for your retirement, it may be that some part of your mind is compelling you to keep up with your neighbors and spend money on the latest gadgets and diversions. Psychologically, you feel like you can't live without those items, even if buying them jeopardizes your future. Most people aren't aware of these thoughts and beliefs, but they are present and influential nonetheless.

*Another universal law: Whenever you believe something to be true, you also believe the reverse to be true.*

Remember Brett's trip to the mall and how most people said that their spouse handled all of the family's finances? This is a great example of whatever you believe, you also believe the reverse to be true. When you are holding on to the idea that only your spouse can take care of the family's finances, whether you know it or not, you also believe the reverse. If your spouse handles all the finances for the family, then subconsciously you also believe that you aren't capable of dealing with it yourself. Now maybe you feel that you aren't educated enough to handle the finances or you simply don't have the time.

If your spouse handles all the finances for the family and suddenly becomes incapacitated or passes away, you may be at a loss. Since you never handled the finances before, you would have no idea about where the money is, what bills are due, whether there is enough money to pay taxes or maintain your lifestyle. Remember that nothing happens *to* you; it happens *because* of you.

Grasping the concept, the reverse is also true, is critical because your actions are either moving you toward your goals or away from them, based on your beliefs. Most of us know someone who seems to continually experience one problem after another. Their life just seems to be filled with crazy events. They are always getting sick and injured, running late for some reason or another, and/or needing money for some emergency. If it weren't for bad luck, this person would have no luck at all. It's as if they have a black cloud of doom circling overhead.

It shouldn't come as any surprise to you at this point that these people are continually creating their own problems. Their internal beliefs might be that there should always be someone there to assist them, possibly because they crave the attention. Subconsciously, they may believe they can't survive without the assistance and attention of others. Until those beliefs change, the continuous cycle will repeat itself again and again, with one "emergency" following the next.

Almost everyone wants to be rich, or at least accumulate a greater amount of wealth than they currently have. And yet, we tend to have negative feelings about wealthy individuals. In the media, they are portrayed as being self-obsessed celebrities, ruthless businessmen exploiting tax loopholes, or children who are obnoxious drug users.

There is a whole industry within reality television of reporters and tabloid magazines following rich and famous people and waiting for them to get into fights, use drugs, go to jail, or behave badly. As a society we watch these shows and find ourselves agreeing with the way these wealthy people are depicted. It lets us draw a vicarious sense of enjoyment from seeing them beaten at their own game or falling from the top of the pyramid.

Against this backdrop, many of us are walking around telling everyone how we don't have enough money. Is it so hard to believe that if, deep down, you really believe rich people demonstrate qualities and traits you don't want to be associated with, you might subconsciously be sabotaging yourself to ensure that you won't become a rich person? You are telling your own mind on a deep level that you really don't have a desire to be rich!

If you have a hard time accepting this idea, think about it a different way. Consider bad habits like smoking, overeating, spending too much, drinking excessively, and doing drugs. We all know these are extremely destructive behaviors that can harm our bodies, and keep us from attaining long-term happiness and success. And yet, millions of people do them anyway, precisely because it provides them with an immediate sense of pleasure. Often, they engage in these activities because other areas of their lives aren't going as well as they would like. They feel upset by their lack of success, abundance, and love, and turn to these vices to forget or feel better in the short term.

Of course, when you put negative beliefs into action, you get predictably negative outcomes. You create a reality in which you continue to experience debt, a lack of savings, and poor business or career prospects. These reinforce the notion that you aren't worthy of being successful, which causes others to treat you as if you weren't deserving, as well.

In reading this, you might be tempted to jump out of your chair and practically scream "I do *not* want other people to treat me disrespectfully! Why would I think that to be true?" Remember that behavior follows belief. If you're willing to disrespect yourself, then you believe others should be able to disrespect you. And don't forget, if you internalize one belief, you also internalize all the others that naturally flow from it. If you feel that it's acceptable to have no savings and large credit card balances, then you believe it's valid for others to treat you as if you have low worth or aren't responsible.

There are literally hundreds of examples of ways we engage in negative behaviors to compensate for things we aren't happy with. In fact, most of us get so much practice that we get to be good at it. For instance, we may show up late for work and then wonder why we didn't get a raise. But should there be any surprise? If you aren't willing to respect someone else's time, then why would they respect your time?

Negative beliefs can even manifest themselves in our bodies. Remember, energy runs through you and is projected out into the universe. Consequently, the energy of your beliefs and thoughts can be made real in your physical self. For example, if you are afraid to move forward in your job or believe it's fine to show up late to work, you may find that you begin having aches, pains, and problems in your knees, legs, or ankles.

Remember, none of us likes to admit we might be wrong, or that we could be the root of our own problems. It's easier to choose not to see, than it is to adopt a new approach and potentially be forced to examine our prior actions and beliefs. That's always painful to go through. But it's necessary if we want to live a life of abundance. No matter how long you've been on a certain road, there's no reason to keep going if it isn't leading you in the right direction. It's better to admit to yourself that you've been wasting your time than it is to continue wasting time.

This message applies strongly to saving for retirement, but also to other areas of your life – eating better, exercising, and respecting yourself makes you a stronger person. If you demonstrate in your beliefs and actions that you are worthy of success, then you will no longer attract poverty *or* health problems.

There are other benefits, too. When we respect ourselves, we no longer look to any other person to give us what we can give ourselves. We stop blaming others. We gain a sense of control.

Take a close examination of your job, your savings, and your finances. If it seems like the variables never change, then realize it's time to look inward for the answers. When you set your lures with the same bait every day, you continually catch the same type of fish. If you hit a golf ball with the same swing, it will always travel in the same direction. When you adhere to the same beliefs and habits, you always get the same results. To get something different and better requires you to make changes inside that will affect your actions and the world around you.

It's time to look at the steps you can take to create the reality and future you desire.

# CHAPTER 11
## SAVING IS NOT AUTOMATIC

It should be clear by this point that you need to be saving money for your retirement, and possibly more money than you previously realized. You should also understand that it's up to you to ensure you are taking control of this process. You shouldn't leave it up to the government, an employer, your spouse, or anyone else. So you're going to have to start doing things differently. But what exactly should you be doing?

Before we answer that question, let me tell you what kind of advice you *won't* find in this book. We're not going to clue you in on specific steps to pay off your debt, how to create a will, raise your credit score, buy life insurance, or offer trading strategies. One reason we're not going to do so, is because your situation is unique. Your circumstances and past decisions have led you to this point and the point you're at now is different than everyone else's. It is impossible to give generic advice that applies to everyone.

Another reason is that we are already buried under tons of financial information. It's not that people can't find the steps to take; it's that they won't follow them. A quick search of Amazon.com reveals that there are more than 1,100 personal finance books for sale that contain the word "steps" in the title. So there is certainly no shortage of how-to advice out there.

Even if you wanted to benefit from it, though, you might run into another problem. Two of the bestsellers on that list are *9 Steps to Financial Freedom* by Suze Orman and *7 Simple Steps to Financial Freedom* by Tony Robbins. Getting your money in order can't be all that difficult if you can do it in just a few steps, right? Look closer, though, and you'll discover that many of the steps that Tony suggests aren't the same ones Suze advocates. Which one is right? Whose steps should you follow?

In reality, it might not matter. That's because you could visit your local library and read all of the "steps to financial freedom" books you want at no charge. They would certainly have lots of helpful information that would increase your financial knowledge base. And yet, you might end up just like millions of other readers – with more *knowledge* than you had before, but the same old financial *habits* that have been holding you back your whole life.

The reason people fail to put their new knowledge into action is the same reason they struggle to lose weight, even though they have the information that eating a salad is healthier than eating fast food. It's one thing to know how to do something, but another thing altogether to alter your behavior in a meaningful way. When an author or expert gives you financial advice that requires you to use your willpower to make many different conscious decisions, they are setting you up for disappointment. To truly build a comfortable nest egg for your retirement, you have to make saving an *unconscious* action.

This idea is simpler than you might think and it's easy to prove if you have a basic understanding of psychology and the mind. From the time you wake up in the morning until the minute you go to bed at night, you probably believe you're conscious of everything that is going on. However, you actually spend very little time a conscious state.

Before you attempt to refute this in your mind, let me prove it to you. If you are sitting down, then stand up for a moment. Ask yourself: how did you stand up? Did you think about the steps involved? What muscles did you use to stand, and which signals did you send to them to turn your ideas into action? The truth, of course, is that none of that happened. You decided to stand up and then just did it. You didn't have to think about the 54 different muscles that were involved in raising you from a sitting position, or the bones and ligaments that had to cooperate. Even though it takes most of the muscles in your body working in concert together just to maintain your balance and remain upright, it all happens outside of your stream of consciousness.

There are a lot of other things that happen "behind-the-scenes," too. Eating, tying your shoes, and driving are all examples of relatively complex actions you probably perform every day without consciously thinking about how you do them. They become automatic through repetition. You weren't born knowing how to tie your shoes, but now you can do it quickly and effortlessly with your eyes closed. You might not even have the conscious thought that you need to tie your shoes. Like so many other daily habits and routines, the act just seems to take care of itself without any effort.

There are other examples of slipping out of consciousness that we could draw on. If you've ever had a workday where the time seemed to fly by, you've experienced a similar phenomenon. When a task that felt like it took an hour actually required three or four, part of your conscious mind essentially stepped back, even though you were probably in a very focused state. It can happen at home, too, where you can become so engrossed in a movie or TV show that you don't realize another person has been talking to you or calling your name.

Although slipping out of consciousness might not sound like a great thing, it's actually quite desirable in many settings. For instance, anyone who plays a musical instrument or a sport will know that this is the ultimate state of mind for superior performance. Following a particularly great concert or show, performers and athletes will happily tell you they were "in the zone". Their instincts took over and every part of their body seemed to be moving in perfect harmony. They hit perfect notes without worrying about their voice, or how their fingers were placed on a guitar. They were able to throw, catch, or kick without much thought.

In those kinds of situations, unconsciousness isn't just preferable, it's necessary. A professional baseball player has only .44 seconds to make contact with a pitch that's traveling towards the plate at 90 mph. If the baseball player first had to think about what kind of pitch it is, when to start swinging the bat, whether he should swing high or low, his mind would react much too slowly and he would strike out. Letting the subconscious take over, the baseball player can now hit the 90 mph fastball on their instincts.

How does this apply to your retirement plan? Just as conscious thinking is actually undesirable for an athlete or musician, consciously thinking about your retirement savings can cause you to miss out on opportunities. You participate in your company's 401(k) plan because you feel like you have to. Everyone else is doing it, or the HR director advises it, so you decide you might as well.

If, you have to make that decision day after day, it becomes easy for you to make other things a priority over savings. The choice to eat out at a fancy restaurant, a night at the movies, or a fancy car, might take priority over saving the money. You need saving to become something that's automatic, just like hitting the fastball would be or tying your shoes.

Fred Bach, author of *The Automatic Millionaire*, tried to teach people the value of consistent saving over time by getting readers to "pay themselves first." In order to do this, he advised setting up an automatic investment plan. In that system, the first hour of a weekly paycheck would be deposited into a 401(k), IRA, Roth IRA, or other savings vehicle. The rest of a person's paycheck would be devoted to bills and expenses.

That's a fine idea, but it's insufficient. If you make $1,000 a week on a normal schedule, then you're being paid $25 per hour. Saving $25 per week is a good start, but it's certainly not going to be enough to give you a comfortable retirement.

Mr. Bach wasn't alone in the realization that savings plans need to be automated if they are going to be simple and unconscious. Even the government has experimented with this approach, enacting laws called Automatic Enrollments. This strategy, which is implemented at the employer level, uses your own laziness against you. It used to be that when you were hired by an organization and informed about your benefits, there was typically a form you needed to fill out if you wanted to participate in a 401(k) or other plan. In other words, you had to sign up if you wanted to benefit.

With Automatic Enrollments, you are added to the retirement package by default unless you complete a form that states you do *not* wish to participate. Assuming you don't make that election, the employer will start deducting two or three percent of your pay automatically and adding it to your retirement accounts. Unfortunately, this has made the problems associated with under-saving in the U.S. even worse. While Automatic Enrollments *do* encourage workers to save something, they also tend to stop them from assuming responsibility for their retirement decisions. Since workers are automatically enrolled in a 401(k) plan, they assume everything is being handled and they don't have to look after their investments. So they don't save above and beyond these plans or manage them actively. As markets go up or down, they don't examine their holdings or make choices that are appropriate for their risk tolerance.

What we can learn from this is that the word "automatic" can be deceiving. It implies that all of the need for decision-making has been taken away from someone's retirement planning. That doesn't help them if they aren't selecting the right funds, fail to contribute enough to meet their employer match, or don't supplement these accounts with other savings.

To make retirement planning work, you don't need someone else to chart your course for you. Instead, you need a set of proven psychological strategies based on science that you can use to set the right habits and stick to them week after week, month after month, and year after year. You need a way to make saving and investing second nature, and something you can perform without an ounce of extra thought. Putting away money needs to be as simple as tying your shoes.

In the Bible, Proverbs 6:9-11 asks, "How long will you lie there? When will you rise from your sleep? A little sleep, little slumber, a little folding of the hands to rest – and poverty will come on you like a thief and scarcity like an armed man." These verses speak to the big problem most people have when it comes to retirement planning: they always think they will have more time to save what they need than they actually will. Nearly everyone says they will start saving more money or paying off their debts next week, next month, or next year. But month after month and year after year, they don't actually get around to it. They remain asleep to the problem, while a future of poverty creeps up on them slowly.

Dean Hankey, in the Foreword, talked about your "M.A.P." He called it your Massive Action Plan, a way to get the RESULTS you want, need, and desire. Instead of calling it a Massive Action Plan, the acronym should be M.A.P.P. and it should stand for **Mindset-Action-Picture-Plan**.

We have already spoken about your Mindset and how you need to change not only your perception but your beliefs. Remember that your actions are directly linked to your beliefs. Thus, changing your beliefs will help you to take better actions.

In the next chapter, we're going to show you how you can start to change your beliefs so that you can so that you can start to take action and create a Plan.

# CHAPTER 12
## THE SAVING HABIT

Baltasar Graacian was a 17th century Jesuit priest who lived in Northeast Spain. Like many priests of his day, he had several interests and specialties. Baltasar was a philosopher, a writer, scholar, and a satirist. In 1653 he published *The Art of Worldly Wisdom*, a collection of 300 short musings on different topics. In one of them he writes:

> *All people idolize something; for some it is fame, for others self-interest, for most it is pleasure. Know a person's mainspring of motive and you have as it were the key to his will.*

Even though this paragraph was written 300 years ago, it remains timeless today. What Baltasar realized, is that we don't always do what we are supposed to do. Instead, we do what we desire at the moment. We all "want" to be wealthy but most of us are not. Thus *"wanting something"* by itself is not enough for you to take action.

As you plot out the route of your M.A.**P**.P., the first P stands for mental **Pictures**. As Dean Pointed out already, there ARE "Good, Better and Even BEST" actions for achievement. Do you buy the latest Smartphone or save that money for your retirement? We don't always choose the best actions. We do this not only because of the beliefs we have, but because we don't know where we are going.

# Picture

The vast majority of us don't have the slightest clue at what age we will leave our careers, whether we will still be working as long as we planned, where we will live in our retirement, or how much we will have saved in our nest egg at that point. We never take the time to think ahead to what we want our future to be, much less visualize it. As Dean Pointed out already, you simply MUST have a clear understanding of "Where You ARE" right now so you can set a path to "Where You Want To Be!"

The first step in changing your beliefs, is to figure out where you are financially. How much do you have in retirement savings? The second step would be to Picture what your lifestyle will be in your retirement. You need to picture it so intensely that you can see it, feel it, and live it in your mind. Figure out what it is you want to do, where you will live, what you will do on a day-to-day basis, etc. Most people haven't given a single thought to what they'll do after their daily careers are over. They assume they'll have some kind of big pension or Social Security income, but beyond that, there is nothing but a vague sense that they'll play golf and tennis, or possibly travel around on cruise ships.

That's not a precise enough image to help you plan for anything. If you want to save for your golden years and avoid poverty, you need to figure out what your life will look like at that point, where you might want to live, and how you'll want spend your time.

To help you get started with this process, we want you to ask yourself some questions and answer them as honestly as possible:

- What would I like to have in retirement that I don't have now?
- What would I like to do in retirement that I have always wanted to do?
- What would I do if money was no object?

- Where do I want to live in my retirement years?
- At what age do I want to retire?
- How much money do I need to achieve my vision?
- How much money do I need to save each month to achieve that vision?

Before you can truly make yourself want to save money for retirement, you have to know what that retirement will look like.

Lewis Carroll, the author of *Alice in Wonderland*, is often credited as having written "if you don't know where you're going, any road will get you there," as part of a conversation between the Cheshire Cat and Alice. Although Carroll's actual dialogue is more complicated than that, the quote *is* a good summary for the way most people think about their retirement savings. It's hard to visualize what you want, if you don't know.

No one can tell you what it should be; the inspiration needs to come from inside you and be as detailed as possible. It needs to represent a clear mental picture in your mind that you can move towards. That's when it goes from being an abstract concept to something you're planning for. Consequently, that's when your subconscious mind starts to turn your retirement Picture into a reality.

Visualization is an important motivational process. Need proof of how important visualization is? If you watch a scary movie, you might be scared. If it's a sad movie you might cry. This is true whether you are watching something or reading something. What you are watching or reading is a fictional story; It's not real. Yet, when the plot line turns sad, you cry. That's because your brain doesn't know the difference.

However you need to do something more than visualize a picture in your mind. If all you do is visualize the nice house, you will have one day, then you are merely day dreaming. You need to bring some meaning to these mental images. Behind your metal picture must have a purpose to accomplish it and that purpose can't be about money. You need to find an emotional reason to accomplish these mental images.

The emotional reason is why you get up and go to work even when you don't feel like it. You go to work because you know that if you don't, you might get fired and would be unable to pay your bills. The pain of running out of money and going into foreclosure keeps you from staying in bed like you might otherwise be tempted to. That's an example of an immediate punishment that motivates you into action.

Let's look at a different example, and one that allows for a little more procrastination. Your taxes are due to be filed on April 15, and if you're like most people, you don't get them done in January. Why? Because there is no pain, stress, or sense of urgency involved. There are months to go, and you feel like you have the situation under control. As the tax deadline gets closer, however, your stress level rises. Eventually, April 14th rolls around and you find yourself sitting at the kitchen table with piles of forms and a shoebox full of receipts. Eventually, the fear of getting fined by the IRS (or worse) is a punishment that forces you once again to take action when you'd rather put off a difficult task.

Now let's look at the habit of saving for retirement. You know you need to do it, but you won't get fired if you don't. In fact, the IRS won't come and ask you about your IRA or 401(k)'s, either. Your friends and neighbors aren't likely to discover you aren't saving either, so there isn't any immediate punishment that forces you to start putting money aside. There is only the abstract knowledge that you'll someday be living in poverty if you don't. In order to turn your saving mindset into a new habit, it makes sense to create a system of immediate punishments and rewards. This can be incredibly simple, but will have huge effects on your behavior.

For example, you might tell yourself that if you don't save $500 this month in your retirement account, you'll have to clean out your garage, paint the house, or perform some other unpleasant task. In order to be motivating, the punishment has to be something you truly don't want to do or have been putting off for a while. The punishment should unpleasant enough so that you'll complete your goal of saving to avoid punishment.

On the other hand, you can also give yourself a reward for accomplishing your goal. This should be something simple, affordable, and not too elaborate. It makes no sense to reward yourself for saving $500 by blowing twice that much on a plasma TV. But, you could settle for something smaller, like a new item of clothing or having your favorite dessert.

One way to give your system of rewards and punishments more power is to make yourself accountable to your friends and loved ones. Social media can be a wonderful tool for this. Go online and tell your friends and family that you've set a new savings target for the month. Let them know what your punishment will be if you fail to reach this goal. They'll be all too happy to hold you to your promise if you come up short, or to praise you when you come through.

Humans, like any other organisms, respond to positive and negative stimulus. You can take advantage of that fact by choosing to give yourself a little push when needed and put you on the path to a more comfortable retirement.

You should spend as much time as possible visualizing what you want as if you already had it. The more vivid the picture and the stronger the emotional purpose, the stronger your desire will be to achieve the goal. Using this visualization tool, you can start to change your beliefs. As powerful your M.A.P.P. is, you will not be able to accomplish anything unless follow the principle of the second P, which is **Plan**.

# CHAPTER 13
## DO THE WORK-CREATE A PLAN

Imagine a world without heart surgery or treatments for blood disease. Certainly we would not have these capabilities if it were not for Charles Lindbergh. Charles Lindbergh was the first aviator to fly nonstop from Long Island, New York to France; by himself. Most people remember him as one of the greatest aviators in history.

Yet, most people forget that he is the reason why Doctors can perform heart surgery. Lindbergh who had no medical training created a heart pump, which pumped blood through organs so that they could be operated on outside the body.

Lindbergh's sister-in-law died of a heart condition. Lindbergh believed that if there was a way pump blood through her heart, while it was being operated on, she wouldn't have died at an early age. With no medical training Charles Lindbergh, along with a French doctor named Alexis Carrel, created a heart pump that would have saved his sister-in-law. Lindbergh had a M.A.P.P. to help create a device to save others. He had the right mindset, he took action, had a vision, and certainly had a long-term plan.

Stop for just a few minutes and imagine how the world would be if everyone had a plan like Charles Lindbergh. Imagine if we all stopped thinking about what is good for me now, and started planning for later in life. How different would the world be if politicians only looked at the long-term impact of laws they passed? How different would the world be if every company didn't think about short term profits, but focused on a long-term plan that would benefit employees and customers?

Successful people are always creating their reality by creating a plan. If there is any secret to their success, it's their long-term focus. They don't approach every business opportunity with fear or short term thinking. Instead today's actions help them to achieve their long-term plans. What do the rest of us focus on? We look to see what is good for us now!

According to the 2015 Insurance Barometer Study, forty-three percent of those surveyed do not have any life insurance. Of those who do have life insurance, twenty percent only have life insurance because it was offered through work.

Most people aren't worried about dying too young, they are worried about paying their bills and maybe saving for the future. However if your spouse passed away without life insurance, saving for the future would be the least of your worries. How would you pay off those credit cards, the car loans, the mortgage, and pay for funeral expenses? Without life insurance, you may have to borrow money from your family just to get by.

When you buy something like life insurance, you are not doing it for the instant gratification. There is little instant gratification in buying something that you may not use. Yet no one would question your action of purchasing life insurance and just to be prepared.

Almost everyone believes that taking care of their family is important. After all that's why you get up in the morning and go to work. As important as family is, most people don't buy life insurance that will take care of their family in the long run. They are too busy thinking about the short term.

Short term thinking isn't limited to life insurance. According the website rocketlawyer.com, seventy percent 70% of Americans with children under the age of eighteen don't have a will. They don't think that not having a will together will have any long term impacts on their family. Legendary guitarist Jimi Hendrix, reggae singer Bob Marley, and pop musician Prince all died without a will. The battle over both the Hendrix estate and the Marley estate went on for 30 years. How can people say that they care so much for their family and not leave any money to take care of their family when they are gone? How can people not leave a will explaining how you want your money divided between family members or who might the guardian be of your children.

We choose not to spend money on life insurance or even spend money for a lawyer to prepare a will. We use our money to buy things that make us happy now. We take these short-term actions for the purpose of medicating ourselves, we want instant relief. The strongest message of every medicine advertised is, it provides quick or instant relief. We don't have patience for a medicine to take more than a few minutes or moments to provide relief.

There is no better example of this short term thinking than the Millennials, the generation born after 1979, who can't imagine ever growing old and who really enjoy spending money. Even though they have the opportunity to participate in their employer-sponsored 401(k) plans, one-third of Millennials choose not to, and nearly half of Millenials admit they are living in the moment rather than thinking about and planning for retirement. The phrase "I'm living for today" is the best way to describe their retirement planning. The Millennials are too busy saving for a new house or a new car to think about retirement; they are preoccupied with now.

Understand this short-sighted view is a mind set and a belief system which we must change in order to be successful in our lives. We are not eager to examine our actions and beliefs to determine how we can change them for the better, because this process takes work.

Jack Zufelt, author of DNA of Success, was raised on an Indian reservation. He was the only Caucasian boy in his high school. They didn't like Jack because of the color of his skin. As soon as school was over, the other kids chased him. If they caught him, he was beaten up and Jack never fought back.

When he was nineteen, he had the opportunity to became the manager of a karate studio and was offered free karate lessons. As discussed in an earlier chapter, Jack decided to **stop blaming others for his inaction**. He decided that he wasn't going to get beat up any more and wasn't going to blame others for his inability to fight back.

His plan to never get beat up again was to throw his heart and soul into karate. For eight years, Jack did the hard work to become a black belt. What work do you need to do? You need to create a plan to change your beliefs about money, create a vision of your retirement, and take action. The path to making change is simple, but not easy. It takes time, patience and a little repetition.

## Repetition

Have you ever wondered why a 30-second Super Bowl commercial can cost almost $5 million? Corporations don't spend that money because they want you to be entertained during timeouts. They do it because they know that, whether you like it or not, you are learning every time you watch TV. The lessons are absorbed more deeply than you might think.

If you were to hear "Don't squeeze the…" or "My bologna has a first name: it's…", what comes to mind? You most likely recalled the Charmin toilet tissue and the Oscar Meyer bologna commercial. If you're a bit younger and don't remember these particular ads, then ask yourself which company is "Like a good neighbor"? What's the commercial that tells you to "Give me a break, give me a break?"

Why is it that you remember these things and can finish the jingles in the space of time it would take you to blink your eye? How can an ad about bathroom tissue be so deeply ingrained in your memory even though it hasn't aired for nearly two decades? For that matter, why do you think State Farm is a good neighbor, or that Jake from State Farm sounds hideous in his khakis? The answer, obviously, is auditory repetition. The more you hear these commercials, the harder it is for you to forget them. Once they are embedded in your brain, you find yourself thinking back to them when you move through a grocery store aisle or go looking for a new insurance agent.

If you are a parent or grandparent, you certainly never sat down and studied the words to the songs they sang on *SpongeBob*, *Barney*, or *Elmo's World*. Yet, there's a good chance you know that SpongeBob lives in a pineapple under the sea, Elmo has a goldfish named Dorothy, and Barney loves you. You didn't try to learn these things, but you couldn't have stopped yourself from learning them if you tried.

Anything that's repeated again and again will form a long-term memory, even if you don't make a conscious effort to memorize the material. So, if you want to change your saving and spending habits, it's not hard to see that you can use the same techniques that advertising agencies use to adjust your thinking.

What are your retirement goals? How much money do you want to save every month? How do you feel about reducing your debt and increasing your credit score? If you want to make improvements in any of these areas of your life, you can record yourself reading your goals into a computer or smart phone. They should be specific and affirming, such as "I will save $500 every month. I enjoy saving money for retirement. I am taking control of my own finances..." and so on.

You could also add some soft music to these recordings in the background if you want, but it's not necessary. All that matters is that you play your recorded goals for a while each day, letting them drone on and on in the background while you drive, exercise, or finish errands around the house. In that way, you'll be reinforcing your desired habits through a subliminal message hundreds or thousands of times per week.

Dr. Maxwell Maltz was a plastic surgeon the 1950s. In the course of his work, he noticed that it would take about 21 days for the patient to get used to their new nose. Eventually, he published his findings in a book called *Psycho-Cybernetics*. After he sold 30 million copies, people everywhere began to think that it takes 21 days to change or form a new habit. Phillipa Lally, a researcher at University College in London, became curious about the often repeated 21 day habit factoid, and decided to conduct a study on the topic. In the *European Journal of Social Psychology*, Lally reported that her participants actually took an average of 66 days to form a new habit.

The reality is it might take you a few weeks to change your behavior, or a few months. However, if you hear your new Mindset, your new Actions, and a description of your vision being repeated many times per day, at some point they will become deeply ingrained into your mind. This is **YOUR PLAN** to help you achieve your retirement goals.

Larry Winget is a six-time New York Times and Wall Street Journal bestselling author. He has been the host of his own A&E TV show, featured in two episodes of CNBCs The Millionaire Inside, as well as appeared in three Hyundai "Dollars and Sense" commercials. Larry was interviewed on YourMoneyShow.com when he wrote his book, "You're Broke Because You Want To Be!" In the book Larry writes, "Books don't make you rich. Sooner or later, like it or not, it always come down to work. If you skip the work, you only cheat yourself and chances are you have been doing that, way to long."

You now have all of the tools to help you create the retirement you desire. Now it's all up to you.

# CHAPTER 14
## PUTTING IT ALL TOGETHER

We have explored a wide variety of pieces to the puzzle of life. We have examined how each piece of the puzzle fits together to create one's reality. One does not get the full view and appreciation of the picture until all pieces of the puzzle are connected.

Achieving the reality you desire takes effort, persistence and faith. However, the results will be greater than you imagined. This process can be as simple as you make it or as hard as you make it.

Examining your actions, thoughts and beliefs takes us on an extremely fascinating and compelling journey. You must be willing to be honest with yourself and face your fears, face your outdated beliefs, and be willing to grow.

Let's review the steps you must take to create the exact reality you desire:

1. **Be Patient**. We live in a society of abundance. Whatever you want is available on the internet. Not only are products in abundance, but they are immediately delivered by the next day. Food is cooked in a microwave within seconds. Want to lose weight fast? Take a pill or get your stomach stapled or rubber-banded. Because of technology, like instant messaging, texting, or high speed internet, we expect everything to happen in our life quicker. When you lose weight fast, it's hard to keep up that pace. Thus when weight

loss starts to slow down, you get frustrated and quit. Remember the story of Ronald Read, the janitor and gas station attendant who left $8 million behind. Ronald spent fifty-six years quietly and patiently amassing his millions. He didn't look to have his grow really fast. He let his money grow over a long period time. Saving for your future requires patience. It's an active discipline. But, with the right mindset, you can do it.

2. **Shortcuts**-As a society, we are always looking for shortcuts. Just look at all of the infomercials on television - Killer abs in just seconds a day! No-money-down real estate! The truth is, there are no shortcuts to success. Even professional athletes gifted with remarkable natural talents practice for hours and hours. Sports legends like Michael Jordan didn't become a sport legend by finding shortcuts. Michael Jordan didn't practice for twenty minutes a day; he practiced intensely beyond the already punishing team practices.

3. **Zero Sum**- That idea is a myth. When someone else wins, you do not lose. If you don't get a promotion, you have not lost out to someone else. You will only have lost if you feel that you will never ever get a promotion. If you experience a setback in your retirement planning, it is imperative to understand you created or contributed to the setback. Examine how you created the setback and take the necessary steps to change directions. Realize that you haven't lost. Realize that you can overcome the setback and maybe it's time to discard those habits and beliefs that contributed to the setback.

4. **M.A.P.P. Your Picture**- In order to go from where you are to where you want to be you must first **PICTURE** what it is you want and make an emotional connection to achieving this goal.

5. **M.A.P.P. Your PLAN-** After you know where you want to go, then you must figure out where you and create a **PLAN** to get to where you want to be. Yes creating a financial plan is part of the planning process. However creating a plan to help you continuously take actions is just as important as figuring out which mutual funds to buy or how much insurance you need.
6. **M.A.P.P. Your Mindset-** Belief is at the heart of everything we do, including retirement planning. Belief has the power to override what we do and say. It also has the power to transform people for better or for worse. Mario Henry played in the NFL for two seasons. After he signed a contract with the New England Patriots he bought a car. He walked into the dealer and showed them his NFL contract. They didn't check his credit or ask him for money. He just walked out of the dealership with a brand new car. After he left the NFL he went to buy a car. He believed from his previous experience that he would walk into the dealership and walk out with a car. Unfortunately, his credit score was poor and he couldn't get a car. Feeling humiliated, he believed that he would never feel that way again. Thus he set out to learn as much as he could about improving his credit score. When you believe in something, you accept it as being true regardless of whether it is or not. You are creating hundreds or thousands of new beliefs everyday. You are even creating a belief right now about this book. People create beliefs about everything including politics, religion, people, food, and many other things. Whatever your belief is, you also believe that the opposite is true as well. If you believe cheating helps you get ahead, then you also believe that you can't survive unless you cheat. Your actions and words will mirror your beliefs.

7. **M.A.P.P. Your Actions-** Your Actions speak volumes. You can't believe one way and act the opposite. Your actions will always follow your beliefs. You can track what is truly important to people by looking at their calendar. For example, you find someone who says that their spouse and their children are important to them. If you were to look at their calendar, you might that they work twelve hours a day and then they play golf on the weekends. Thus their family cant be as important as they say. Most banks have a website that will create a budget for you and show you where you spend your money. When it comes to saving for retirement, you can track what is truly important to people by looking at this budget. Are the credit cards at their maximum limit? Are the bills paid on time? Do they live beyond their means? If the answer is YES to these questions, it means that something else is more important to them, like getting the most advanced cell phone, the newest computer, an expensive car, etc.
8. Know **It Was You All Along**. Once you appreciate the full magnitude of your ability to create everything in your life, you will begin enjoying each experience. Like Sherlock Holmes, or a crime scene investigator, you will attack each experience with passion to understand the depth of your beliefs. You may laugh at yourself as you discover some strange, tightly held belief realizing the impact this one belief has created for you.

Investigating how you were drawn into a particular event or into someone else's life is even more fun. Being drawn into another person's life is even more magical. If in a dark moment you believe you do not have anything to offer others, simply step back and notice all of the people's lives you have touched, remembering that each person asked for you to come forth to help them discover the depth of their experience. You must believe you can have it all. You must believe in the universal truth that you create it all. You must believe there is something better for you than what you can see with your present limited perception.

You must not take "no" for an answer; in fact negative thoughts are not part of your thought process.

You can have it all. So what's stopping you from starting?

# CHAPTER 15
## SO WHAT'S STOPPING YOU?

So what's stopping you? What is holding you back from creating the nest egg you have so long desired? You may have many reasons why you believe you won't succeed. You may have suffered some financial setbacks, had a difficult childhood, you believe that you are not smart enough, or maybe have already tried and failed.

You may believe your circumstances are different from everyone else, preventing you from ever being able to save money. You are correct. Whatever you think about you bring about. If you believe your circumstances prevent you from saving, then that becomes your reality. In reality everyone's circumstances are unique, special and different to each of us. We all have our own mountains to climb, emotional scars to manage, physical and mental challenges, and unsuccessful or incomplete attempts at achievement.

The problem is that we tend to make excuses instead of using the power each of us is given to change the future. How many times have you said "I don't have the time to learn about saving or the money to save?" Guess what you are not alone. Most people tend to procrastinate because they believe they don't have the time or money. You may believe that keeping the status quo means you have not made a choice. However not making a choice, is still a choice; and you have given away your power.

Maybe you're sitting on the sofa and eating to make yourself feel good, when you know you should be doing a budget, looking at your investments, or learning about finances. You rationalize sitting on the couch by convincing yourself that "I worked hard today, I need a break, watching a little TV and having some cookies couldn't hurt." The list goes on.

When we aren't procrastinating, we are focusing on the negatives. "What if I fail?" Isn't it fascinating the majority of people first think of failure? Remember walking on the wooden plank 30 stories in the air? The images of failing opens to more negative thoughts which freeze us in terror. Yet, is there such a thing as failure?

Success is rarely, if ever, accomplished in one attempt. Have you ever watched an infant attempt to take his/her first steps? He/she will pull themselves up against something, holding on tightly to the sofa or chair, only to fall back down again. Does the child give up after a few tries? Stop and strongly consider that if we all gave up after a few tries, none of us would be walking and running today! This is no small accomplishment for a baby. In their world learning to walk is similar to us to obtaining as large of goal we can imagine.

The infant is relentless in their attempts and does not quit. Instead the infant — even one so young — figures out what went wrong, makes adjustments and tries again. Nowhere in the infant's head is the idea of failure.

At no time does the child believe that they will never be able to walk or believe that they will be criticized by their friends. None of these beliefs enter the mind of a child. Only adults have these negative beliefs when trying to achieve goals.

So how do you stop procrastinating and start making changes? Your finances are dictated by what you believe. When you switch insurance companies it's because you believe you are paying too much for your insurance. You make changes in your life because you believe your life is out of control. Your taxes are due on April 15th and, if you're like most people, you don't get them done in January. Why? You believe that there is no pain or stress; no real sense of urgency. With taxes you can get them done at the last minute. However, with saving for retirement, it's hard to do at the last minute.

Popeye the Sailor Man is the spinach eating lovable cartoon character, created by E. C. Segar in 1919. With his adopted son Sweet Pea and his girlfriend Olive Oyl, Popeye is constantly being picked on by Bluto (aka Brutus in later comics). Every episode Popeye finds himself in a bad situation. Just as when it seems hopeless Popeye yells, "That's all I can stands, cuz I can't stands no more." Then a can of spinach falls out of his shirt or pops out of his pants. Popeye immediately eats the entire can of spinach and Popeye is blessed with superhuman strength.

When it comes to finances, what is it that will make you say, "That's all I can stands, cuz I can't stands no more." What in your financial life do you believe has caused you to be so fed up? Often times when we are fed up with our finances, we look for a big score. We want to hit home runs. We play the lottery and the stock market to win the big one. We want to take big steps all at once. Baby steps are for babies.

While we are working hard to create the one big deal, we overlook all the small steps we can take to help us create the world we desire. Every day we can hit "singles" to get us where we want to be. Home runs are sexy, popular and exciting. Singles are boring. Yet in the long run, be patient and hitting singles day after day, is very productive.

Remember in an earlier chapter about taking shortcuts? The key is to work toward your goal consistently and in small steps. Go for singles, not the home runs. You can hit a single every day. Opportunities arise for you every day to hit a single. Who do you think created those opportunities? You did. We have a tendency to overlook opportunities when they present themselves. Our attention can be so riveted on the big step that we miss the chance to obtain your goal one small step at a time. As we have discussed in earlier chapters, many people do not have the patience to take it one small step at a time.

Now, it's all up to you, because it was your retirement, all along

www.ingramcontent.com/pod-product-compliance
Lightning Source LLC
Chambersburg PA
CBHW070305230526
45470CB00002B/728